PSYCHOTIC ANXIETIES AND CONTAINMENT

PSYCHOTIC ANXIETIES AND CONTAINMENT

A Personal Record of an Analysis with Winnicott

Margaret I. Little, M.R.C.Psych.

JASON ARONSON INC.
Northvale, New Jersey
London

Library of Congress Cataloging-in-Publication Data

Little, Margaret I.
    Psychotic anxieties and containment / Margaret Little.
      p. cm.
    Includes bibliographical references (p.
    ISBN 0-87668-785-0
    1. Psychotherapy—Case studies. 2. Winnicott, D.W. (Donald
Woods), 1896—1971. 3. Psychotherapy—Study and teaching—Case
studies. I. Title.
RC465.L57   1990
616.89′17′092—dc20   90-712
                                               CIP

Manufactured in the United States of America. Jason Aronson Inc. offers books and cassettes. For information and catalog write to Jason Aronson Inc., 230 Livingston Street, Northvale, New Jersey 07647.

Contents

PART II
On the Value of Regression
to Dependence

CHAPTER 1

Introduction by James S. Grotstein

We are in Dr. Little's debt for her sharing the history of her personal analyses with us. Her report of them is of enormous importance to psychoanalysts and psychotherapists because of her first-hand experience with emotional depths many of us have either never had to traverse or never had sufficient guidance to be able to be conducted through such an inner Purgatory that we only dimly realized lay within us. Her recording of her three analytic experiences is of special value since she, too, is an analyst and shares with us her experiences in three different kinds of analysis: Jungian, classical Freudian, and object relations. This rich comparative experience reminds one of Nini Hermann's *My Kleinian Home,* in which she, too, had

had three different styles of analysis but differed in
terms of the third, a Kleinian analysis.

Dr. Little offers us an acute vicarious perspective of
a transference psychosis, one that differs from a
transference neurosis by virtue of the cataclysmic,
disorganizing regression that takes place in the
former. This quality and depth of heart-rending and
mind-rending experience have rarely been subjec-
tively reported with such poignancy and clarity, especially by an analyst. She clearly outlines for us the
infantile and childhood roots of this psychosis and
enables us to see its intimate transference fluctua-
tions, which Winnicott's "good-enough" and sometimes "not-good-enough" holding environment allowed to develop. One gets the impression from
reading both Winnicott and Little (in this and in her
other noteworthy contributions on the subject, especially *Transference Neurosis and Transference Psychosis*) that a "position" must be addressed that
either accompanies or antedates that which Klein
designates as the "paranoid-schizoid position" and is
one that requires "environmental provision." Winnicott expanded Freud's, Abraham's, and Klein's con-
ceptions of early infantile existence by apparently
taking the primary narcissism that the first two
espoused and the inchoately separate and needy
infant that Klein espoused and combining them into a
dyad of the passive "being" infant (the normal prototype for the "true self") who needed intuitive (and
silent) "holding" and the "active," "doing" infant
(the normal prototype for the "false self") who needed
to search for and utilize the breast. It would appear,
consequently, that Dr. Little's "being" self had to be
intuitively located, gathered, held, and allowed to
heal so that she could be prepared and "outfitted" for
the controversial rigors and phantasies, first of the
"paranoid" relatedness to the object, and then of the

"stage of concern" (Klein's depressive position). In other words, there is a stage of primary at-one-ment (primary narcissism: "There is no such thing as an infant. There is only a mother and an infant.") side-by-side with the separate needy infant. The first needs both to be found and also never to be found, one of the profound dialectical paradoxes that run through Winnicott's works. In being found, it knows that it is loved and is meaningful to mother *without having had to ask! Thus it is affirmed!* Insofar as it is unfound, its innocence, privacy, and uniqueness are left inviolate. It is allowed both to "be" and to create the objects of the world that provided for it in time for it to believe that it has created—and then discovered—the object. It is then safe to allow itself to need its created/discovered mother's breast, from which experience issues the "spontaneous gesture," Winnicott's own definition. Not only did Winnicott allow for a dual track for infant development; he also allowed for normal omnipotence, which he often called "illusion," and he dealt with the pathology of its absence in his conception of privation and deprivation. He dealt with the pathology of its presence in "fantasying," which he thought of as pathological omnipotence, as opposed to "fantasies" apposite to the internal world, which he thought of as the normal counterpart to the world of external reality and distinctly separate from "fantasying." He conceived of the space of interaction between the infant and its mother—and simultaneously of the space between the infant and its spontaneous creations—as "potential space," which then defined the space for analytic regression. I have gone into some length about Winnicott's concepts because Dr. Little has given us such a rich demonstration of him at work with her where these ideas seem to stand out.

We are indebted to Dr. Little also for another favor

she has done us, that of giving us an intimate picture
of how Dr. Winnicott conducted her treatment, how
he interpreted, how he did not interpret, how he
offered her a "holding environment" or "environmental management," how he helped her create a
"potential space" for creative illusion, how he kin-
dled and fostered her interest in "transitional objects," and glimpses of him as a human being who
discreetly shared with her items of his own life and
health of which he believed she should be apprised.
She illuminated for us how he dealt with anger (his
and hers) and other forms of aggression, especially
self-assertion, which he seemed to be keen to foster. I
was especially interested in the fact that he chose
only one patient at a time for a deep regressive
treatment. That was all he could handle. The other
patients had to wait their turn. How he was able to
stave it off in those patients waiting their turn is
incomprehensible. I was intrigued as well by the
implication that Winnicott, as Little portrays him,
seemed to believe that one of the inescapable consequences of this deep cataclysmic regression in the
patient was a corresponding regression in the analyst, who should also rigorously maintain his/her
healthy observing ego. This may be the reason why
Winnicott chose to handle only one deep regression at
a time.

Thanks to Dr. Little, we now have a glimpse into
Winnicott the analyst, Winnicott the healer, and
Winnicott the person. Winnicott seldom revealed his
actual technique with adults except in short anec-
dotal segments. *Holding and Interpretation: Fragment of an Analysis* (1972) is a notable exception. Dr.
Little's account is unique in that it reveals Winnicott's technique from the perspective of a seasoned
professional psychoanalyst *and* patient. One easily
gets the impression from reading Little and Winnicott

that the latter is truly the father of the concept of the "therapeutic alliance." He seems to have comported himself with Dr. Little in a way that was similar to his descriptions of mother–infant interactions—that of a *partnership* rather than that of a breast-infant-feeding hierarchy, as was (and is) the case with Kleinian thinking.

The work of Winnicott and his followers (he would have bristled at that term since he eschewed being "followed" or idealized) is now becoming welcomed on a greater scale than ever before. Long known largely for his concept of transitional objects, the holding environment, and primary maternal preoccupation, the analytic world has awakened slowly but surely to the fact that, despite his deceptively practical language and despite the fact that so many of his contributions were delivered to lay audiences, he was not a "British Dr. Spock" but rather a sophisticated and sentient metapsychologist whose contributions have plumbed the ontological depths of our existence, have "transitionalized" psychoanalytic perspective from the single subject to the indivisibility of the dyad, have introduced the "third dimension" of dialectics, irony, and paradox into a psychoanalytic theoretic structure that did not know that it was still trapped in the "first dimension" of "either/or," and helped to legitimize the therapeutic (and therefore positive) aspects of countertransference. His concepts of privation, deprivation, and impingement gave precision and clarity to the introjective consequences of pathological parental caretaking and laid the foundation for object relations deficit theory. Winnicott (1965) stated, "Psychosis is environmental deficiency disease" (pp. 135–136). His concept of the "antisocial tendency" anticipated self psychology's later obsession with issues of *entitlement,* and, furthermore, along with the contributions of Fairbairn, laid the foundations of the concept of the narcissistic and borderline personality disorders, including the vertical split ("true self"/"false self") and horizontal split (conscious/unconscious).

There are other reasons why he has not been better appreciated until now, at least in Britain and in the United States, notwithstanding the fact that the popularity of his work has steadily developed in France, Australia, South America, and other areas. His ideas developed in part as a consequence of his relationship to Melanie Klein. At first a pediatrician and then a dedicated classical analyst, he became deeply impressed with and immersed in Klein's then revolutionary ideas. Klein meanwhile had gotten caught up in"ecclesiastical" debates of great bitterness with the Vienna School generally and Anna Freud specifically, which continued past the deaths of each—in one of the most dreadful, shameful, and regrettable chapters in the history of psychoanalysis. The "war" caused such polarization that Klein, like Freud long ago who demanded signs of loyalty from *his* followers, demanded strict adherence to her ideas as privilege for membership in her group. Klein and Riviere denied that Winnicott's work was of any value. They asserted it was the result of illness in him (Rodman 1987, letter 25). Also, there was a contrast between Klein's and Winnicott's view of the degree of ego development in the neonate (Winnicott 1962e, chap. 16). Winnicott, thoroughly immersed in and appreciative of Klein's work, bristled at the need to submerge his own ideas in conformity to hers and also had substantive differences with her, not merely over the issue of reality per se, but over its inclusion in psychoanalytic theory and technique.

Thus, Winnicott had been caught in a polarizing war, could not take sides, and, along with several other British analysts—like Fairbairn, Balint, Bowlby, Khan, Little, Milner, and others, who also, although predisposed toward Klein—could not foreswear their belief in the *technical* importance of reality. He became part of the so-called British object relations school, which today is called the Independent Group. As I recently reread the entirety of Winnicott's published works, I became impressed at how Kleinian was the basis of his orientation, but I became impressed also at what an innovator of Klein he was. What seems to distinguish his work (and the work of other members of the Independent Group) is the prime importance of the relationship of reality to fantasy, the latter having an uncompromised role of importance in Kleinian theory and the former being the counterpart and instigator of phantasy for the Independent group.

Winnicott, for whatever reason, seemed to have grasped that deficient and impinging parental practices had a disruptive effect on infant development over and above Klein's conception of mere parental release of innate infantile destructiveness. This is a subtle but important issue for psychoanalysts, and I should therefore like to address it at some length. One of the legacies of Freud's second theory of psychoanalysis (his first was the repression of a traumatic sexual memory) was that of the inherent sense of guilt that the human being acquires from birth because of his/her inevitable and inexorable phantasies of excessive appropriation of the person of one parent and of murderous aggression toward the other parent, i.e., the Oedipus complex. The outcome of this second theory for psychoanalytic technique was to shift the emphasis from reality to phantasy and, furthermore, to shift the *sense* of responsibility for one's emotional illness from the outside to the inside—i.e., the patient had to accept that, no matter how badly one had been treated as an infant or child, one's *responses* to the neglect or impingement were the only significant elements of importance for psychoanalysis. The rationale for this seemingly unilateral and ascetic perspective was the putative need for the patient to "own" his/her own reactions to the neglective and impingement traumata of his/her upbringing rather than to blame, and therefore to self-absolve prior to ascending to one's own acceptance of one's ontological (existential) self. In other words, when all the complex metapsychology was discounted, the infant-patient needed to "own" his/her responsibility for his/her dilemma in order to "know" him/her self. What had all along been assumed in psychoanalytic theory but not sufficiently explicated was that Freud's second theory of psychoanalysis issued from the putative hermeneutic perspective of the infant, whose narcissistic proclivity impels him/her to account (hermeneutically) for all happenings in external reality as occasioned by impulses from within him/herself, not yet having the maturity to account for a world separate from the self that has a separate agency of causation.

Winnicott was very aware of this classical Freudian perspective, which had become all the more emphasized in Kleinian technique, but he also had the experience of being the Medical Director at Paddington Green, a hospital and clinic for children, and observed first-hand the interaction between mothers and infants. His elaboration upon Klein, therefore, was a corrective one from his perspective, not a dismissive one. He emphasized the nature of the relationship between the the nursing couple and the importance of mother's acceptance of the primary at-one-ment with her infant, her ability to soothe, to care for, and to dedicate herself to its survival and thriving. What he seems to have been aiming at was the importance of the background launching of this new human being, the "environmental provision," "holding environment," etc.

Winnicott seemed to have emphasized that the infant was not an infant without its mother and therefore helped to launch a major shift in psychoanalytic focus from the unitary self to the indivisible relationship between two (mother-and-infant), which has become the well-spring for self psychology. Furthermore, his concepts have dovetailed with those of Bowlby and of Stern. Perhaps one could accurately epitomize Winnicott's approach as follows (which constitutes a restatement of what I have said above): The infant-patient's "being" self must be prepared by an environmentally providing background ("holding environment") to become a striving, needy, desiring, "doing" self who is capable of a transference neurosis with oedipal conflicts. Failing that, the analyst must become the veritable substitute for the absent holding environment of the past and must prepare the patient for a "neurotic analysis" by his very holding.

Winnicott was advocating in a sense what Searles had termed *symbiotic relatedness.* I believe the essence of that point of view is one that approximates "healing" and that may transcend "therapy." What is left for us is to validate Winnicott's and Searles' positions and draw guidelines for sharing, touching, conversing, helping—for being a friend!

Margaret Little was apparently the victim of frightened and unattuned parents but was the beneficiary of one of the great "healers," let alone "therapists," of psychoanalysis. We thank her for revealing a portion of his method.

I

Winnicott Working in Areas Where Psychotic Anxieties Predominate— A Personal Record

Polonius	for to define true madness What is't but to be nothing else but mad?
Hamlet	I am but mad north-north-west, when the wind is southerly I know a hawk from a handsaw.

William Shakespeare, Hamlet, II. *ii*

CHAPTER 2

The Risk of an Account of My Own Analysis

Psychoanalysis is nothing if not dynamic, being concerned with human instincts and drives, and the anxieties to do with them; a human activity, revolutionary in its beginnings, and not always smooth in its evolution.

Changes, new ideas of theory or technique have aroused profound anxiety, and often brought about divisions such as those early ones when Jung, Adler, Stekel, and others broke away from Freud. Later, in our British Psycho-Analytical Society, the work of Melanie Klein provoked controversy, anxiety, and the tendency to defend against it by denial and strengthening of resistance, as before.

Freud found that where anxieties were concerned with the oedipal situation—castration, loss of part of the body, loss of an object or of self-esteem—a transference neurosis was developed in analysis, and could be resolved. But where anxieties concerning existence, survival, or identity predominated (narcissistic neuroses and psychoses), transference neurosis did not develop and psychoanalysis (in its classical form) was ineffective (Freud 1913).

In the course of time fewer people have sought treatment for neurotic illness, and many more for anxieties of the far less tractable, psychotic type, even though these were not necessarily wholly incapacitating or requiring hospitalization, and this has called for changes in psychoanalytic thinking and technique. Winnicott, following his work with Melanie Klein, and applying knowledge derived from his long study of infants, children, and their parents, has carried out the treatment of a number of patients with psychotic anxieties, and his work, in turn, has brought anxiety and controversy, for it shows a more human face of psychoanalysis than that usually seen before. There is much true interest in his work, and a wish to know and to understand it. There are also, however, criticisms—both friendly and hostile, and often ill-informed—as well as straightforward curiosity and voyeurism.

Winnicott's work with children is fairly well known by now. He wrote systematically and talked about it freely, and many people were able to see him in action at Paddington Green or one of his other clinics. In treating psychoneurosis in adults he used "standard technique" (Winnicott 1962d), analyzing transference neurosis and being concerned with the Oedipus complex and the development of the superego.

But in treating adults a very high degree of confidentiality was needed. Some of his patients were colleagues or students in training, and some were prominent or well-known people. Consequently, he has left us relatively little information, and a good deal of such clinical material as he has written up seems to me obscure and difficult, for he used a kind of *oratio obliqua*—"the patient indicated . . . and I interpreted that . . ."—rather than direct statement—"He said . . . and I said . . ." There are small pieces of clinical material scattered throughout his writings (Winnicott 1947–1971) describing and explaining everything that this paper is about, but no whole account of any one patient. Thus for anyone who only read his papers and had no opportunity for discussion, it would be very difficult to form a realistic picture of what he actually said or did.

I can best show his work by giving an account of my own analysis with him—clinical material that has always been recognized as essential for the development and understanding of theory and metapsychology, which I am perhaps in the unique position of being able to supply. (Freud used material from the analysis of his own dreams.)

Winnicott's work is based clearly and definitely on certain principles. Its hallmarks are: recognition of the importance not only of the individual human being himself, but also of his earliest environment; empathy (understanding nonverbal communication and body language, far beyond the recognition of unconscious movement, posture, etc.) and experience of mutuality; consistency without rigidity; allowing "regression to dependence" (Winnicott 1954a, b); "holding" (Winnicott 1962b, 1963f) and play (Winnicott 1971b).

This is a far more difficult undertaking than anything I have attempted before, for I start out knowing only too well that I cannot hope to do justice to my subject. I am also aware that I cannot avoid arousing a considerable degree of anxiety in some readers, especially those who adhere closely to classical theory and practice, though others—colleagues, former analysands, and nonanalysts—who have encouraged me in writing this, will welcome it.

Apart from the limitations of time and space, unconscious mechanisms lead to all sorts of distortions, including falsifications of memory. As well as my wish to clarify, therefore—to do away with misconceptions and misunderstandings as far as possible—I have to reckon with my own narcissism and exhibitionism, my inhibitions and my more realistic reticences.

I have thought about it all long and deeply, and have put off the attempt for fear of utter failure, but I have decided at last that I must take the risks and pains involved and make the best fist I can of it, or something really valuable will go to waste.

Giving this account involves writing of my history and my family, and of treatment by two other therapists, one a Jungian, the other the late Ella Freeman Sharpe. I tell it as I *experienced* them, being as objective as I can, but introducing, inevitably, a slant that others may well dislike or disapprove. (Ibsen wrote in a letter to Björnson [1865], "If I cannot be myself in what I write, then my work would be nothing but lies and humbug," and that is how I feel.)

It is an account of human beings, men and women, in human activities, conditions, and relationships. And since men and women are apt to do things well or badly, to behave oddly, to make mistakes, to feel and show in one way or another widely ranging emotions, even to be "mad north-north-west" (*Hamlet*, II. ii), both light and dark sides of those concerned are here to be seen. I hope that both *will* be seen, for either alone is meaningless. ("Care shall be taken not that the [reader] . . . may understand if he will but that he must understand whether he will or not"—

Quintilian, *Institutio Oratoria*.) It is worthwhile stating here that despite the difficulties, despite the human limitations, the outcome is one that both Winnicott and I found satisfying, one for which I am profoundly thankful. (Light excelleth darkness—Ecclesiastes 2:13, Authorized Version.)

I am presenting the material chronologically as far as I can; it falls into three divisions with these three quite different people. In each case I can mostly give only the general *feel* of what happened, and a few isolated episodes that stand out, for I seldom recorded anything.

CHAPTER 3

Psychotherapy with Dr. X., 1936–1938

In 1936 a woman friend who lived with me was persuaded to seek psychotherapy. She had broken down in 1933 following what she understood to be lesbian advances made to her by a colleague.

For three years I had endured long bouts of weeping and sulking, accusations, and suicide threats that I believed to be serious. She would flounce off, drive madly on the motorway, and hide for hours, coming back only late at night when I had given up trying to find her. And I had a busy general practice to run at the same time.

As soon as she started in treatment I knew that I needed it too, and set out to find it.

Despite the fact that for the whole of the first three weeks I was so paralyzed with fear as to be unable to speak or move on the couch, Dr. X. never regarded me as being more than mildly neurotic. He *recognized* the overwhelming tension without pretending to understand it, and eventually released it by gently massaging my belly. He treated me as a rational human being, and implied that I could be attractive as a woman—which I had never believed possible, though somehow I knew myself to be heterosexual. He encouraged me to train as a psychotherapist at the Tavistock Clinic, and took me as his guest to meetings of the Medical Section of the British Psychological Society.

Not everything that Dr. X. did was helpful, but he enabled me to break free from my clinging and dominating friend and establish a different relationship with her, largely by pointing out that she had the right to kill herself if she so wished, that it would be final, and that in fact I could not prevent it. Several minor symptoms, mostly somatic, cleared up during the treatment with him.

I recall few things from the two years (three sessions per week) with him. He remarked one day, "You seem to be always thinking of other people and apologizing for your existence, as if you thought you had no right to it." I had indeed thought that, but he explained that I *had* the right, as I had not been responsible for it. I told him that my earliest memories (aged two) were of being obviously "in the way" and "a trouble" when my sister Ruth and my mother and I all had whooping cough. I was in a cot in the corner of the room where they were in bed together. I coughed and vomited, my mother got up to hold me, and they both started coughing, "as if I had made them." And later, one day my father came in, in a hurry for his midday meal, and finding the room strewn with nappies and pot and toys, and me

coughing and vomiting in the middle, he said angrily,
"Can't you *stop* that child being sick?"

In the last session before a Christmas break, Dr. X.
wished me well, but added, "For the love of Heaven,
be yourself." (?"Don't be that vomiting child.") I
replied, "I don't know how, I don't know what *myself*
is." He met my parents socially, and he and my father
got on well. My mother asked for a consultation, and
he said afterwards that he "couldn't stand her," but
did not enlarge on this. The treatment came to an end
gradually, without difficulty, he assuring me that I
needed no more analysis, but only "synthesis,"
which presumably I could work out for myself. A mild
friendship followed as I was no longer a patient but a
colleague.

He knew Ella Freeman Sharpe personally and gave
me a friendly introduction to her. I went to see her at
her home, in 1938. Dr. X. had himself had a very
short period of analysis with a member of the British
Psycho-Analytical Society, "so as to know how it felt
to be an analysand."

CHAPTER 4

Psychotherapy with Ella Freeman Sharpe, 1940–1947

When I went to visit her on Dr. X.'s introduction, I had an experience that terrified me because of its implications. I "saw" her in a kind of grey mist, like a spider in a web that was her hair. I knew it at the time to be delusional—a spider "of the mind" (*Macbeth*, II i). I told her that Dr. X. had said I "needed no more analysis," only synthesis, and I literally *ran* from the house in panic. Yet at the same time there was a strange attraction to her and a feeling that I would have to see her again some time.

Late in 1940 I found myself emotionally involved with a patient and decided that I could not go on treating him. Dr. X. was not available, and in great anxiety I sought out Miss Sharpe, as the only psychoanalyst whom I had met.

My disturbance was profound; psychoanalysis for me meant total annihilation, and my fear conflicted with a deep sense of longing. She had a vacancy, and started straightaway, and the fear at once became unbearable.

In the first session I lay rigid on the couch, again unable to speak or move. Then, as she remained silent I began to scream, "This *can't* be real," recalling my earlier near-hallucinatory vision of her and my flight. It felt like a nightmare. At the end of the hour she said, "Get up and sit there, and let us talk." She interpreted my fear as "castration anxiety" and related it to my having met her through Dr. X., which was, of course, the obvious thing, for the problem I had taken to her was clearly oedipal. But this did not fit the *intensity* of my panic, which was far more than any mortal terror, or fear of death. For her, mortal terror meant fear of the (classical) superego, to which "good" is equated with nonsexual, and "bad" with sexual.

My fear—"such dread that children only can feel" (*Jane Eyre*, Chap. 3)—was of utter destruction, being bodily dismembered, driven irretrievably insane, wiped out, abandoned, and forgotten by the whole world as one who had never been—"cast into outer darkness" (Matthew 22:13).

Her papers on the technique of psychoanalysis (Sharpe 1930) give a clear account of her way of working, founded on the idea that psychoanalysis is wholly concerned with infantile sexuality in all its forms, i.e., relating to the Oepidus complex, and with repressed phantasies about the parents that can only be recovered via the transference neurosis. Patients must not be allowed to use reality as a defense against these; the analyst's integrity consists in his asking of himself everything that he asks of his patient; existence is justified by allowing the right to it to others.

My terror in that first session (see Sharpe 1943) being expectation of total annihilation was part, not of a transference neurosis, but, as I came to realize much later, of a transference psychosis, based on actual experiences from childhood and earliest infancy.

The overall picture of my analysis with Miss Sharpe is one of constant struggle between us, she insisting on interpreting what I said as due to intrapsychic conflict to do with infantile sexuality, and I trying to convey to her that my real problems were matters of existence and identity: I did not know what "myself" was; sexuality (even if known) was totally irrelevant and meaningless unless existence and survival could be taken for granted, and personal identity established.

Freud (1913), writing of narcissistic neuroses (melancholia) and psychoses (schizophrenia and paranoia) had made clear the distinction from sexual neuroses (psychoneuroses) in that in the two former, only ego instincts, survival, and identity are concerned, and that transference neurosis is not developed. (Transference psychosis was not recognized at that time.) Freud (1917) also found in them no ambivalence but only a fixed hostility that made analysis impossible.

A transference to Ella Sharpe *of some kind* had clearly been formed and was assumed to be a transference neurosis, as it was in part. My hostility to her became fixed as a result of her inability to see the true nature of my anxieties. But there was ambivalence, the positive elements being released by her pattern of altered behavior to me off the couch, as she describes (Sharpe 1930), treating me as if I were "a guest" in

her house. Then she was very kind and warm,
friendly and generous, so bringing about just the split
situation that Freud had described (Freud 1913). For
me this brought back exactly the confusion and
ambivalence that I had experienced with my mother,
so that in my psychotic areas Miss Sharpe became
identical with my mother (Little 1959), who had not
been able to provide an environment where it was
safe to *be*; Miss Sharpe's aim was to provide one
where it was safe to be *sexual or hostile*. I *was*
hostile, and defiant, but it was not safe; I became
compliant, and dependent on her as I had been on my
mother from infancy. My dreams at that time of
struggle, confusion, and fragmentation were interpreted as phantasies of violent coitus and repressed
wishes to have intercourse with my father and to
destroy my mother.

About six weeks after we started I told her that I
would like to train as an analyst. She encouraged me
to apply, and after interviews with Dr. Edward Glover
(then Chairman of the British Psycho-Analytical Society) and Dr. Payne (the Training Secretary) I was
accepted, and she continued to encourage me,
praising my work and my other activities.

But our struggle still went on. I spoke once of how
I wanted "to be somebody," meaning to be a real
person, not nobody, or an un-person, as I felt I was.
This was interpreted as my wish to take my mother's
place, to *be* my mother bodily, in her sexual relationship and reproductive capacity. What I truly dreaded
was that I might find myself to be a "cheap second-
hand copy" of my mother or of her (which amounted
to the same thing), but I could not get this across to
her, or that the risk was real. Whenever I spoke
of either of my parents what I said was, for her,
phantasy, and any reference to the realities was

taking refuge. So I was doubly caught in the "spider's web"; *I* was the crazy one, not my mother; *she* was the one who "knew," as my mother, not I, had always known; while *my* recognition of my own and my mother's psychosis was dismissed as phantasy. I was once again in the confusing "Wonderland" or "Looking Glass" world of my childhood, where simultaneously I "imagined things" and "had no imagination," where I could not *but* know what I saw and knew, and "didn't know anything."

Always on the couch reality had to be set aside, including observations of her age and her health, and specifically of her heart condition. It was not only my "prerogative" to say whatever came, I was bound by the "analytic rule," so I spoke of what I could not have failed to recognize as signs of longstanding heart disease, cyanosis, and clubbing of her fingers. She made no reply, so I knew this must be secret and forbidden, and in making a "personal remark" I was automatically being "rude."

I, much younger and in good health, was not allowed to help but had to stand by useless, while she, who was in danger of heart failure, dragged a heavy couch from one end to the other of a long room, at every session. (My mother used to say I was "spineless, always taking the line of least resistance." "What use would *you* be on an Arctic expedition?" and quoted Milton "On his Blindness.")

In November 1945 both my parents were taken ill suddenly; my father was delirious and unmanageable. His condition was diagnosed as "cerebrovascular accident," needing treatment in hospital; accommodation being difficult then, it had to be a mental hospital. He died there five days later of broncho-pneumonia; post mortem showed his brain to be intact.

His illness and death became the center of a major family disturbance. Ruth, having first refused to share a room with me, asked me to go away. My mother ordained that there should be no flowers at the funeral, to which she could not come. It was a bleak affair attended only by one of my brothers and myself. (Later, she showed her possessiveness and unconscious hostility to him by allowing nothing more than the bare notice of his death to appear in the magazine of the school where he had taught for thirty years.)

I was due to read a paper for full membership of the British Psycho-Analytical Society a week after his funeral. I wanted to put it off, but Miss Sharpe insisted that I should read it. Between my immediate distress and my psychotic transference I could not stand up to her, but I felt it as a massive interference with my mourning.

I read the paper and enjoyed the discussion. She was pleased with my success, and beyond a simple, obviously sincere expression of sympathy for my loss nothing more was said about either my mourning or the family upset. The analysis went on as if nothing had happened except my reading my paper.

My unwillingness to read it then was interpreted as due to guilt about my envy of her ability to write and present papers, transferred from my parents in their sexual relationship and creativity, and fear of retribution if I dared to assert myself or to challenge her in any way. I could not deny the envy, but I felt it to be relatively unimportant at that point. (I gave a disguised account of this in my paper entitled "Countertransference and the Patient's Response to it" [Little 1950].)

In April 1947 we agreed to terminate after the summer term."There is no point in going on analyzing for the sake of analyzing," she said; but in May, at the Whitsun holiday, she died suddenly.

I had attended and enjoyed the first postwar Conference of European Psychoanalysts in Amsterdam. I had made new contacts and new friends, and for the first time been aware of a man's interest in me. I had said goodbye to Miss Sharpe on my birthday (which was also my father's) a few days earlier, and she had wished me many happy returns. I returned to the news of her death.

So, here was a repetition of the earlier trauma of my father's death, which had never been worked through, the reality having been all but denied at the time; and this had repeated an even earlier trauma, when I had been similarly prevented by Miss Sharpe from mourning the loss of an aunt whom I had loved, and instead, been given a transference interpretation about her coming holiday, which felt as illogical as most of my mother's "explanations."

I went to see Dr. Payne, and on her couch I raved and wept wildly for an hour. At the end of it she said in tones of surprise, "But you're very ill!" I replied, "That's what I have been telling Miss Sharpe for the last six years." I knew that my real troubles had never been touched; instead of empathy there had been "confusion of tongues" (Ferenczi). Feeling more a nonperson than ever, and knowing no more than before what "myself" was, I was once again fully exposed to my psychotic anxiety, with overwhelming rage, guilt, helplessness, and despair.

Dr. Payne referred me to Marion Milner, who helped me on general analytic lines and supported me generously for the next year or so; but the situation was difficult as we had been students at the same time. Then D.W. had a vacancy and took me over.

During this time my old friend and housekeeper

had to retire. I made an important move of house, separating home and consulting-room and living alone for the first time. I also embarked (for the first time) on a sexual relationship with a man, for me hitherto impossible.

CHAPTER 5

Psychotherapy with D.W.W., 1949–1955, 1957

So, thirteen years after first seeking psychiatric help, and now aged 48, I came to D.W. I cannot give as clear, coherent, or detailed an account of the time with him as I could wish. I can only recount some of the things that happened.

My previous acquaintance with him had been slight. The first scientific meeting of the British Psycho-Analytical Society that I attended was on a noisy evening with bombs dropping every few minutes and people ducking as each crash came. In the middle of the discussion someone I later came to know as D.W. stood up and said, "I should like to point out that there is an air raid going on," and sat down. No notice was taken, and the meeting went on as before!

I heard him speak at other meetings and read

41

papers. Then, at the end of the evening in 1945 when I read my membership paper, "The Wanderer: Some Notes on a Paranoid Patient," which he had not discussed, he came and asked if I would take a child patient. I was very pleased to be asked, but regretfully said No. I had recently finished analysis with a child, for training (in child analysis) which I never completed. It had aroused enormous anxiety and I felt badly about the way I had ended. I was in turmoil about this, about my father's death and the circumstances surrounding it, and could not consider dealing with another child just then, but I left it open for the future.

I heard him read his papers "Reparation in Respect of Mother's Organized Defence against Depression" (Winnicott 1948b) and "Birth Memories, Birth Trauma, and Anxiety" (Winnicott 1949b) and felt that this was someone who could really help me.

The preliminary interview with him was short, perhaps fifteen minutes. At no time did he take a formal history of any kind, but feeling his way, built up gradually his understanding of what was troubling me and of my "heart's need" (George Eliot, *Mill on the Floss*). I made my sexual affair an excuse for not pursuing the analysis; he accepted this but said that he would keep the vacancy open for the time being and I could take it up later if I wished. It was not long before I went back to him, as I found the sexual relationship difficult.

The first session brought a repetition of the terror. I lay curled up tight, completely hidden under the blanket, unable to move or speak. D.W. was silent until the end of the hour, when he said only, "I don't *know*, but I have the feeling that you are shutting me out for some reason." This brought relief, for he could admit not knowing, and could allow contradiction if it came. Much later I realized that I had been shutting myself in, taking up the smallest possible amount of space and being as unobtrusive as I could, hiding in the womb, but not safe even there.

In one early session with D.W. I felt in utter despair of ever getting him to understand anything. I wandered round his room trying to find a way. I contemplated throwing myself out of the window, but felt that he would stop me. Then I thought of throwing out all his books, but finally I attacked and smashed a large vase filled with white lilac, and trampled on it. In a flash he was gone from the room, but he came back just before the end of the hour. Finding me clearing up the mess he said, "I might have expected you to do that [clear up? or smash?] but later." Next day an exact replica had replaced the vase and the lilac, and a few days later he explained that I had destroyed something that he valued. Neither of us ever referred to it again, which seems odd to me now, but I think that if it had happened later on he would probably have reacted differently. As it was, it felt as useless as my struggles with Miss Sharpe or my mother, and I forgot it until recently. Many years later, long after termination, when asking for advice about a very disturbed patient who hurt me knowingly and repeatedly, I spoke of having hurt him. He agreed that I had, but added that it had been "useful."

Some weeks after this, throughout a whole session I was seized with recurring spasms of terror. Again and again I felt a tension begin to build up in my whole body, reach a climax, and subside, only to come again a few seconds later. I grabbed his hands and clung tightly till the spasms passed. He said at the end that he thought I was reliving the experience of being born; he held my head for a few minutes, saying that immediately after birth an infant's head could ache and feel heavy for a time. All this seemed to fit, for it was birth *into a relationship*, via my spontaneous movement, which was accepted by him (Little and Flarsheim 1964). Those spasms never came again, and only rarely that degree of fear.

He soon found that for the first half of every session nothing happened. I could not talk until I found a "settled" state, undisturbed by any impingement such as being asked to say what I was thinking, etc. It was as if I had to take into myself the silence and the stillness that he provided. This was in such contrast with the disturbances of childhood, my mother's anxiety-driven state, and the general hostility from which I had always felt the need to retreat to find quietness. From then he extended the length of the sessions to an hour and a half, at the same fee, until nearly the end of the analysis.

Here I feel it is appropriate to speak of the two things about which there has been most misunderstanding—*holding* and *regression to dependence*. D.W. used the word *holding* both *metaphorically* and *literally*. Metaphorically he was *holding the situation*, giving support, keeping contact on every level with whatever was going on, in and around the patient and in the relationship to him.

Literally, through many long hours he held my two hands clasped between his, almost like an umbilical cord, while I lay, often hidden beneath the blanket, silent, inert, withdrawn, in panic, rage, or tears, asleep and sometimes dreaming. Sometimes he would become drowsy, fall asleep, and wake with a jerk, to which I would react with anger, terrified and feeling as if I had been hit. He has himself described such sessions (Winnicott 1970b). He must have suffered much boredom and exhaustion in these hours, and sometimes even pain in his hands. We could speak of it later.

"Holding," of which "management" was always a part, meant taking full responsibility, supplying whatever ego strength a patient could not find in himself, and withdrawing it gradually as the patient could take over on his own. In other words, providing the "facilitating environment" (Winnicott 1965), where it was safe to *be*.

Only rarely did holding mean literally restraining or controlling. He was compassionate, but consistently firm, sometimes to the point of ruthlessness where he felt it necessary for the safety of his patient. Short of bodily intervention he could "forbid" action. This was powerfully effective, for although it might be disobeyed it could not be unnoticed, because it had been said and also because in the context of a delusional transference (Little 1957b) it became automatically the patient's own prohibition, and then joined up with some element of sanity (Little 1959). It worked on both conscious and unconscious levels.

Sometimes the holding had to be delegated, handing over a dependent patient temporarily to someone else so that he could get rest, or a holiday, but always keeping in close touch.

During one of his holidays he arranged, without my knowing, for a friend of mine to invite me to join her and two others in Switzerland: later, when he feared that I might kill myself while he was away, he arranged for hospitalization. (I will come to this again.)

At one time I was liable to rush out of his room in a fury and drive away dangerously. He took charge of my car keys until the end of the session, and then allowed me to lie quietly alone in another room, till I could be safe. He emphasized the need to "come back" (Winnicott 1954a) from the deep regression to ordinary life, for "regression to dependence" means regression to dependence for life itself—to the level of infancy, and sometimes even to prenatal life.

All of this, of course, was built up on his wide knowledge and understanding of children of all ages, and of parents, recognizing the need for support and for someone *to be there*, to take responsibility. His always growing capacity for empathy, being in touch with id, ego, and superego, in people of all sorts and all ages, including himself, understanding body language in all its forms, was an essential part of him. He did not defend against his own feelings but could allow their full range and, on occasion, expression. Without sentimentality he was able to feel about, with, and for his patient, entering into and sharing an experience in such a way that emotion that had had to be dammed up could be set free.

I told him of an early remembered loss. I had found a friend, "A.," at school, someone who had chosen me to be *her* friend. She had made me free of her home, her nursery, her Nanny, and her toys. One day after a holiday she wasn't there, and then for many days she was "ill"; and then she was "dead." I had been "unkind" and "selfish" in not writing to her. I "couldn't have cared," or I "would have written." He found himself in tears—for me—and I could cry about it as I had never done before, and mourn my loss.

"Why do you always cry silently?" he asked. I told him I had learned that early. Once, crying with toothache at the end of a long day which had been trying for everyone, I was told. "Do stop crying, darling, you make everybody else miserable," and next morning, when the abscess had burst in the night and the pain was gone, "You see, it was all a fuss about nothing." And often, "Cheer up, darling! You'll soon be dead."

This made him very angry. "I really *hate* your mother," he said. He was "shocked" when I told him how till the age of 10 and over I had to "rest" every afternoon in a darkened room with no toy or book, and was shamed when I had gnawed the candle by my bed until it had a waist and I could get small fragments of wax that I could chew and squeeze and mold.

I found D.W. essentially a truthful person, to whom "good manners" were important; he had respect for the individual, whether patient or colleague, though he could be outspoken in criticism. To demand "associations" or to push an "interpretation" would be "bad manners," as well as being useless. He was as honest as anyone could be, responding to observations and answering questions truthfully unless there was a need to protect another person, but it was essential to *know* when his answer was not wholly true, and why.

He would answer questions directly, taking them at face value, and only then considering (always with himself, often with the patient) why was it asked? Why then? And what was the unconscious anxiety behind it?

I was allowed to work at my own pace, and he adapted himself to it. Only when some circumstances —usually unforeseen and external—made it necessary would he put on pressure. This was very important for me. It allowed me to be myself, to have a pace that was my own, whereas at an early time I had been alternately pushed and held back, so that neither the pace nor the inconsistencies were mine.

The timing of the full regression could not be mine alone: it depended to a large extent on his case load. He spoke of patients having to "queue up" sometimes to go into such a state, one waiting until another had worked through it and no longer needed him in that way. But it was mine in so far as it could not be until I was ready.

He gave very few interpretations, and those only when I had already reached the point where the matter could become conscious. Then of course the interpretation would ring true. He was not "infallible," but often spoke tentatively, or speculated: "I think perhaps . . . ," "I wonder if . . . ," or "It seems as if. . . ." This let me taste or feel what he said, and be free to accept or reject it. Interpretations were not given as if I had access to symbolic function where I had not.

One day his secretary told me that he was not well and would be a little late for my session. He came, looking *grey* and very ill, saying he had laryngitis. I said, "You haven't got laryngitis, you've got a coronary. Go *home*." He insisted that it was laryngitis, but he couldn't carry on; he rang me that evening and said, "You were right, it *is* a coronary." This meant quite a long break, which was very painful, but at last I was *allowed* to know the truth: *I* could be right, and I could trust my own perceptions. It was a landmark, and he knew it.

He had said of me a little earlier, "Yes, you *are* ill, but there's plenty of mental health there too." I began to react with anxiety, and he added, "But that's for later on, the important thing now is the illness," having recognized my fear that he would deny or lose sight of it. Later he described me as being "like a person suffering from multiple sclerosis whose brain was involved."

This was a very true picture of my "borderline" state, and of my transference to him (Little 1964a), for the lesions in multiple sclerosis are scattered, and cerebral involvement brings patchy mental distur-

bance; and there were, as I knew, "patches" of illness
and of health. They also reflected my mother's state,
as he spoke of her. "Your mother is unpredictable,
chaotic, and she organizes chaos around her" (see
Winnicott 1961). "She's like a Jack-in-a-box, all over
the place." This had indeed been my earliest environment from which I could not separate myself despite
my father's stability and reliability, for her chaos
affected him too. D.W. later commented that I would
probably have been all right if I had been removed
early to the care of a stable foster-mother. (I should
perhaps emphasize here that despite my difficulties I
did not give an appearance of "abnormality." I had
attended school, passed exams, even won scholar-
ships; I had qualified in medicine, run a successful
general practice, and trained and qualified as a psychoanalyst. Also, except for three periods each of
about eight weeks, plus holidays, I worked continu-
ously as an analyst, throughout my analysis with
D.W.)

A note about my family is needed; otherwise much
of what I say is difficult to believe or understand. I am
surprised to find how little I actually told D.W. about
it *in words*, yet his comment about my mother was
like a revelation (not an analytic "interpretation"). It
made it possible and allowable for me to understand
much of what I already knew, things I had observed
or been told.

My mother's childhood, in Australia, was *horrific*,
with an alcoholic and unstable father and a loving but
dominating, meddlesome and unpredictable mother,
to whom my grandfather was unfaithful. Two older
brothers, one of whom my mother adored, both
teased and petted, frightened and bullied her. A
younger brother was born blind, and at the age of 5,
she was made responsible for looking after him when

another child was born. Nearby were the frightening world of the convict settlement from which my grandfather drew his labor force, the cannibal Aborigines, and the Bush where children were often lost, and seldom found.

My mother had to be brave, amusing, and clever. Her father too teased, petted, and bullied her, and finally disowned both her and his blind son. She learned to dance for him and kick over the brandy bottle "accidentally," also to defend her mother in parental quarrels. This is not the place for all the details that I know, but she told me shortly before her death that she "could only live at all by turning everything into a game" (see Searles 1959). The wonder is that she *did* live at all, to marry my father who was as devoted to her as she to him. That was never in doubt, though they teased each other and their children often quite sadistically. Her idea of sex was "an unpleasant duty that a woman owed her husband"; childbirth was sheer horror, warded off by padding her body so that her pregnancy could not be perceived, and avoiding labor (which would inevitably be fatal) by "not thinking about it" until this became impossible. Being afraid was "cowardice," "contemptible."

My father was by no means a nonentity. He was a mathematician, who gave up prospects of a university career and became instead a schoolmaster, to pay his college fees (unpaid through his father's bankruptcy). He was stable, warm, and companionable, but all his relationships and outgoing activities (yachting, golf, etc.) were systematically destroyed by my mother; only solitary pursuits or those involving his family were tolerated, and he became irritable and short-tempered. He was overconscientious, inhibited, and shy with women, and undemonstrative with his children. The only woman he was ever known to speak to was my mother; it was love at first sight and for life, and he could seldom stand up to her.

Small wonder then that all their children were disturbed in some degree. She expressed her fear that each one would "turn out badly." My elder sister, Ruth, brilliant intellectually, developed a savage superego and considerable moral courage and power of endurance. She became a legend in her lifetime, and a saint; sadly, for her, "This life would not be worth living if there were not to be a better life hereafter." My younger sister, Cecily, became ill immediately after my parents emigrated to Australia (always the Promised Land) in 1934, and died (aged 28) almost before they got there. (They stayed only four years.) My two brothers—uni-ovular twins ten years younger than I, born prematurely after a near-fatal pregnancy, to a mother aged 42 who already had three children—are both alive and they have had their difficulties.

To Ruth I was "an irritant," and I must have been a threat to her supremacy, for I was sickly both as a baby and later, needing and getting a lot of attention, probably owing to congenital hiatus hernia together with coeliac condition (both genetic), which have troubled me all my life, neither being diagnosed until my late sixties. (Before that, of course, my complaints were "fuss," or "imagination" and later "psychogenic," but always something that I "should control."

My mother did her level best to be a good wife and mother, sometimes successfully, but anxiety made her a compulsive meddler, possessive and always interfering in other people's concerns and relationships. She was a highly intelligent and gifted person, warm and loving, but in a wholly uncoordinated way, being tragically damaged. The only predictable thing was that she would be unpredictable; one had to live with it and find ways of dealing with it. The only play possible—whether with toys, balls, or words, etc.— had to be hers; it was often good, but any play of my own would either be stopped or taken over. Spontaneity, "idea, impulse, action. . .all one. . .together, knowing what to do" (Sacks 1985) was aborted. Her own mother, the benevolent tyrant, was never far away, and not always so benevolent.

My blind uncle was almost the only person I could ever talk to. He was a scholar, widely read, musical, and very independent. When he married I lost all contact with him and became deeply depressed and physically ill.

During my analysis with D.W. I went through three periods of serious depression during which I was unable to work. I had long been aware of spells of depression lasting about ten days, at intervals of about three months, quite apart from any known loss, which I had never understood. And there had been two incapacitating depressions that followed losses that I knew.

Early in the analysis, after a severe attack of gastroenteritis (which I recognized later was a flare-up of the coeliac condition), I went on feeling very ill and exhausted physically and deeply depressed. I was not able to go for my sessions. D.W. came to me at home—five, six, and sometimes seven days a week for ninety minutes each day for about three months. During most of those sessions I simply lay there, crying, held by him. He put no pressure on me, listened to my complaints and showed that he recognized my distress and could bear with it. As I recovered physically the depression gradually lifted, and I was able to work again.

Psyche and soma for him were not separable, they

were "body and spirit which deep down are interde-
pendent aspects of the same reality" (van der Post
1982). He was always concerned for my physical
state; he kept stethoscope, sphygmomanometer, and
clinical thermometer handy, and used them. He
would advise me to see my G.P. or a consultant if
necessary, but he would also take my word for my
own condition. Once, when I had a mild bronchitis,
he questioned whether I should not go to my G.P., but
I told him, "I'm not ill. I'm unhappy." And that was
enough.

The time from the autumn of 1950 to the spring of
1952 was a particularly painful one for me. I had
come back from my summer holiday with an appoint-
ment fixed to see D.W. again, but found that he had
had a second, though less severe, coronary, which
again meant a long break.

Then, I was asked to be assistant to the Business
Secretary of both the British Psycho-Analytical Society and the Institute of Psycho-Analysis, taking two
years to prepare to take over. After attending only
three meetings of the Board and Council I knew I did
not want this, but the next week my predecessor died
suddenly, and I was left with it. I was "the obvious
person" to succeed her, and the pressure on me to
undertake it was so great that I could not refuse.

This was when the move from Gloucester Place to
Mansfield House was being planned and carried out. I
was by far the most junior member of the Board and
Council of which D.W., as Training Secretary, was a
member. I disagreed with much that was decided,
and I came to detest the job and everything to do with
it. I tried to convey that a *trained* Secretary was
needed. I felt guilty, futile, and inadequate and
wanted to resign, and I became ill again. Although it
was a great relief when at last, in May 1952, I was

replaced, and soon a trained Company Secretary was appointed, the guilt and depression persisted, especially as I found that there was now no place for me to take part in the training scheme, whereas at the time of Miss Sharpe's death I had already been invited to do so. (In fact, D.W. told me that he had intervened to forestall it because I was "too ill.") Also, in 1951, following publication of my paper "Counter-transference and the Patient's Response to it," I had been invited to go to Topeka as a training analyst but had had to refuse as I was deeply involved in my analysis.

At the same time as my unhappiness about all this I was in great anxiety about D.W., who was himself depressed after his coronary. It was like a childhood year, when I was in difficulties at school due to a mistake about my age, and simultaneously in anxiety at home on account of my mother's pregnancy. I don't think we spoke of his depression at all, but I was aware of it (as with Miss Sharpe) from his altered appearance and manner, for every analysand is sensitive to what is going on in his analyst.

I was always afraid that he would have a third coronary and die, which would have been fatal for me. One day when I went for my session I waited to be told that he was ready for me. Several times I asked the receptionist, "Is he still not here?" Finally, after forty-five minutes, I went to his room expecting to find him ill or dead and found he had fallen asleep on the couch and not heard the bell! So I was saved, and again I was allowed to know, and to follow my own impulse. But my depression continued, and at the lowest time I could not sleep at night until I had phoned D.W. ringing repeatedly until he answered.

I learned afterward that both his second coronary

and his depression came about through his distress about the question of breaking up his first marriage—a decision which he did not take lightly. Eventually he told me of his divorce and coming remarriage, lest I should hear of it elsewhere or read of it in the press. I found it difficult, especially as my own love affair was finally falling apart. I was very jealous, and some oedipal material could be worked through, though it remained as an isolated patch that had to be joined up later.

My sessions went on as before, but now at his new home. The analysis seemed unending, and I blamed him for my failures. But then, in the summer (1952), for the first time in my life, I *exploded* at my mother, at some piece of her jibing and "clever" nonsense. I told her exactly what I felt: that she was being unkind and ridiculous, that she had had no business to marry or have children, and a great deal more in the same strain, quite regardless of any effect on her.

D.W.'s comment was, "You've owed it to yourself for a long time." It was an important spontaneous self-assertion that had never been possible before, and although I did not see her again until she was dying, two years later, I have never regretted it.

His holiday and mine came. I went to the far north of Scotland, to wild country where I walked by myself. My mother wrote making an outrageous demand; my "explosion" was ignored and made useless, her possession of me reasserted. I *stomped* furiously up a steep, slippery, and remote mountain path in a thick mist. Next day, still raging, I slipped on wet grass outside my hotel, fell, and broke my ankle. (Had this happened the previous day I might well have lain all night before being found.) I was taken to hospital and cared for; my leg was put up in

a light plaster over a gutter splint. My postcard to
D.W. telling him of the accident brought a telegram in
reply, and a letter.

The Medical Superintendent of the hospital was
most helpful. He spoke of the depression that follows
sudden loss of mobility, having experienced it himself as a young man, when he had polio.

At the end of a fortnight I was beginning to get
about and was discharged. But then came the difficulty of getting home. My car and other things were
sixty miles away in one direction, my home six
hundred in the other! Fortunately, two friends I had
made in the hotel came to my rescue, one dispatched
the car to me, the other invited me to stay in her
home, which was on my way, until I could arrange
my own journey and the car transport.

By the time I reached home the plaster was loose
and had to be replaced. The new cast was heavy and
unwieldy with a rocker badly placed under the heel,
so once more my mobility was greatly restricted and
walking precarious.

When I saw D.W. again six weeks later, so many
things had happened that I was confused and had lost
all contact with what had triggered off the accident
and so never told him about it. He assumed that it
belonged wholly to the transference, to do with his
holiday (cf. Miss Sharpe's reaction to my mourning),
also that it was a serious suicidal attempt. I might
have protested, but the fresh loss of mobility had
renewed the depression, and I suppose there was
unconscious guilt about my verbal attack on my
mother, my refusal of her demand, and the physical
attack I had surely wanted to make but had turned
against myself.

I find I have no recollection of the content of the
next year's work in the analysis, so I think I must

have projected the confusion, etc., and D.W. must have taken it over (Searles 1959), otherwise it is difficult to understand what followed, in particular why the hospitalization and regression that had already happened consequent on the accident were apparently not used as fully as they might have been.

As I understand it now something *had* to be broken—to free me from my mother's hold and to destroy finally the pattern of repetition. Two childhood memories belong here. One is of her gripping both my wrists, and saying emphatically, "You *must* control *yourself!*" But in fact *she* was controlling *me.*

The second is of being ill with pneumonia — part of an early "breakdown" (aged 5) brought about by massive sudden changes including a move to a new house, where my father was in charge of school boarders; overnight there were nineteen boys, to none of whom I was allowed to speak. At the same time there was a change of kindergarten. I had not liked the first one, but I detested the second, where I was teased by a boy older and bigger than myself. (A year earlier Cecily had appeared overnight, and I was moved to share a room with Ruth, who teased and frightened me.)

At the new kindergarten sexual identity was confused. In a singing game of "Birds in a Nest" the "father bird" was a little boy with long fair curls like my own, dressed in a frock, and with permanently running nose (uncontrolled). But he was a "boy," and I a "girl," so I couldn't have been the "father bird." ("Men and boys have short hair and wear trousers; women and girls have long hair and wear skirts," I had been told!)

Now, suddenly ill with very high fever and delirium, I was moved to my mother's bedroom and my father moved out. The content of the delirium has never been recalled as such, but I think it must have been concerned with these questions of freedom to be myself and of sexual identity.

My mother's account is that I clung to her night and day and would not let her go. D.W.'s understanding was that "She would not let you die"— which was true (as I learned later) but now I would say: "She would not let me *choose* whether to live or die." I *had* to live, for her.

So, when she reasserted her hold on me after my "explosion," something had to break and it was my own ankle.

I was tied by the leg again on my return from Scotland. The confusion then was a repetition of the delirium in which I could not distinguish between my mother and myself and literally did not know what "myself" was. Being in this confusion meant that I could not make clear to D.W. what it was about, or what had happened to precipitate it, any more than I had been able to make my mother understand the earlier confusion (or to stop vomiting). Then, I had only been able to be ill and threaten to die. D.W. too could not let me choose whether to live or die, and he did not realize that I had already made my choice unconsciously, in falling where I did.

So when the next summer holiday lay ahead, D.W. told me that he wanted me to go into hospital as a voluntary patient, "to make sure that I did not commit suicide." I went for him, wildly; I think I hit him, though I am not certain. He caught my wrists and held me, and was not hurt. Eventually I agreed, on condition that he would ensure that I was not given electro-shock, that I could have a private room, that I could discharge myself if I wished (make my own choice), and that he would take me there himself and bring me back—all of which he agreed and carried out. He made it clear that he would also keep in touch with the hospital.

We went on the day after the International Congress in London (1953) ended. On the station platform he found that I was clinging to the edge of his raincoat, terrified. He took my arm in his, and when we arrived he said, "You're being very brave," and added something about "innate creativeness," which I did not understand and do not remember, but later found had been important as relating to spontaneity.

He was distressed that the Medical Superintendent had gone on holiday, not having told him this before. The Deputy was a hard man, antagonistic to analysis and not too pleased to be given extensive notes and an absolute ban on ECT!

At first when D.W. had left me I felt protected, but after a few days forlorn and abandoned. I was confused and slightly disorientated. (I made notes from day to day of those five weeks, which I still have.) For ten days I kept to my room, weepy and afraid, but to my surprise I began to write poetry.

Then, one morning I asked and was promised to be left alone and undisturbed. One after another, no less than eight people came, and when the eighth, a ward maid, was on the floor by my bed I spanked her bottom. Immediately the Deputy-Superintendent came. I felt he threatened me; there were "other ways of treating mental illness besides analysis which were sometimes necessary." I reminded him of the ban on ECT. By the evening I was full up with anger. I let fly at my supper tray; I hurled the reading lamp and anything I could find across the room in an orgy of smashing. I was promptly secluded for the night, and all night long was paranoid, seeing the nurses who came as "devils." But I had clung to two things that later proved to be "transitional objects" (Little 1950),

a handkerchief that D.W. had given me and a soft
blue woolly scarf that I had liked and bought. In the
morning I was moved to an open room in a locked
ward, and the ward Sister came. Later, bathed and
fed and cared for like an infant, I was settled in the
room where I stayed for the rest of the time.

In my sessions with D.W. there had been "token"
infant care; he always opened the door to me himself,
each session wound up with coffee and biscuits, he
saw to it that I was warm and comfortable, and
provided tissues, etc. But here was the full "regression to dependence," an extension of what he had
given me; and he kept in constant touch with the
hospital and sent me postcards letting me know
where he was.

The hospital care was total and interference mini-
mal; everything was provided and no demand made.
I spent the time sleeping, reading, writing, and painting, sometimes on the walls of my room; playing, in
fact. I wandered in the garden and roamed the
streets; when it rained a ward orderly would fetch me
in with umbrella and waterproof. When my feet were
blistered the Sister dressed them and told me, "You
should have telephoned for a car to fetch you."

There might be distress or disturbance going on
round me but the place went on *being*, and holding
and looking after me, calm and apparently unper-
turbed. (Nothing could have been more different in
that way from my early environment. I recalled a day
in 1944 when Ruth and I were both visiting our
parents; there was no time when all four of us were
sitting down together for as long as five minutes, for
something had always to be fetched or done. It
couldn't have been quite so bad earlier, but then I
would have been less well able to cope with it than I
was now.)

Something had again been broken (plates, lamp, etc.) but not *me*, and I was now in what had become my real "nursery," where it was *safe* not to control myself. The boundaries were wide and flexible. It was psychically an extension of D.W.'s consulting-room where, earlier, I had smashed his vase. I could now make clear *to myself* my choice between life and death ("To be . . .or . . . not to be"—*Hamlet*, III. i, *pace* Winnicott 1971b). His putting me in hospital was a repetition of his reaction to that earlier smashing, but this time the contact was not broken as it had been then, when he left me alone with the wreckage I had made.

It was only much later that I realized that the wreckage *itself* was a creation, for destruction and creation are inseparable—you can't paint a picture without destroying a white canvas and tubes of paint (and everything has ambivalency), "for there is nothing lives but something dies, and nothing dies but something lives" (Thompson 1924), and "love involves destruction" (Winnicott 1963b).

Though there were plenty of things I didn't like in the hospital, overall it was kind and cozy, and at times even fun. One day I painted a sea, and added suddenly a huge monster's head emerging, with flaming eyes and fierce jaws. It was pinned up, and the occupational therapist stood looking at it with his back to me. I said, "A nice piece of schizophrenic art, what?" He shot out of the room and down the corridor, and the Sister came in chuckling, "What *have* you done to poor Mr. Y?" she said. "He looked as if the devil was after him!" And we laughed together, not at him, but at my painting. Spontaneity was restored, and even welcomed.

But I couldn't have accepted living so for long. That I had to be there at all depressed me further, and one day seeing a bit of rope in the garden I thought again of suicide. All at once I realized that it would be no real solution, only a victory for the crazy world I had struggled against all my life and too often complied with (Winnicott 1963b), and a really mad act. I never considered it again, and I came back from the regression to ordinary life (Winnicott 1954a).

I started work about a fortnight after going home . My analysis had begun to move toward termination. There was plenty to tell D.W. about the time in hospital, working through the experience, talking over the content of my paintings and poems, telling of my play and my phantasies much as a child would tell its mother. I still sat up half the night painting wild pictures and writing melancholy poems. D.W. would look at them and comment. He was not critical or judgmental though he would say what he *felt*, and it was some time before I realized that his disliking a picture didn't mean I should destroy it. It had a value simply as a creation, for him as well as for me.

At some point in this terminal phase D.W. gave me one particularly important interpretation that had the same quality of "revelation" as had, earlier, his observation about my mother's "chaos." He told me that such fear of annihilation as I felt belonged to "annihilation" that had already happened: I *had been* annihilated psychically, but had in fact survived bodily, and was now emotionally reliving the past experience. It was some time before I could assimilate this and use it (Winnicott 1968). Even now I tend to forget it in times of stress, but as soon as I recall that interpretation the anxiety is relieved. ("Dread is only memory in the future tense" — Elizabeth Ayrton, *Day Eight*); and "Survival is the twin brother of annihilation" — Churchill, Speech in 1941.)

It was true that I had been annihilated, before I

even existed. I was not a person in my own right, only an appendage of someone else: introduced, "This is my daughter"; known as, "Ruth's sister"; one of three Margarets in my class and two M. Littles in the school. My second name, Isabel, was useless too: "It's always *I,I,I*," I was told, and in trying to get rid of the self-centeredness I discarded the initial, and have only used it lately to distinguish myself from another psychiatrist of the same name!

By now the character of the sessions had largely changed, for so much grief and pain and anger had been worked through that play, the ground of creativeness (Winnicott 1971a), could take its place and the relationship born years before could develop. There are analysts who apparently believe that every session *ought* to be painful, but while D.W. was fully aware that analysis could only work for someone who really suffered, he believed in the value of a relationship that could also be encouraging and enjoyable. Quite a lot of the play through which I now grew psychically *could* have been like my mother's: jokes, stories, and nonsense (I once asked him why he had chosen to join the Navy rather than Army or Airforce: "The uniform suited his blue eyes better"!), bits of gossip, information, and serious discussion about analysis. But these things were not used to defend against anxiety, to ward off anger or excitement, or to deflect pain or unhappiness by making me laugh. They were not forced on me, I could have them or not as *I* wished. Being *human* was the all-important thing and play an essential part of human life at any age.

D.W. could let me see something of the demands that such an analysis as mine made on him, demands that he was willing to meet, and not only on condition that the analysis should succeed: standing

anxiety, guilt, pain and grief, uncertainty and helplessness, standing what couldn't *be* stood. There was
no defense against paradox or ambivalence, whether
in a patient or in himself. He told me of one patient
who for many months had threatened suicide seriously enough for him to arrange hospitalization. The
suicide happened, unnecessarily and for the wrong
reason as he felt, because his instructions had been
ignored. He had gone through a long period of anxiety
before it, and guilt because he hated the patient for
making him suffer (Winnicott 1947). He wanted to
scream, "For God's sake, get on and *do* it." When it
did happen, there were fresh guilt and helplessness
(he should have been able to prevent it), fury with
those who had failed to carry out his instructions, and
finally a deep sense of loss of someone about whom
he cared intensely and in whom he had invested so
much feeling.

All the same, he made it clear that total self-
sacrifice was just not on. If he did not care for himself,
providing for his own needs, bodily and emotional, he
would be no use to anyone, including himself. Hence
the importance of his marriage, holidays, music,
friends, etc. I came to see changes in him, growth and
development, alterations in his way of working: in-
tangible things perceived only after they had happened. I once spoke of regretting that I had not come
to him earlier; he answered that he could not have
done my analysis earlier.

His letting me share something of this made it safe
for me; it increased my own sense of being valued and
therefore valuable, and so my ability to value myself
could build up. I became aware that the D.W. whom
I knew was different from the D.W. known to anyone
else, even though others might know some of the
same aspects of him. I "created" him imaginatively
for myself, and this because they and I were different,

however much we might all *seem* alike; it gave them their values and reality. Above all, D.W. became a real living person with whom I had a relationship born years earlier and no longer based only on transference.

Other relationships followed with colleagues and friends. Early in 1954 my mother died; I had not seen her or Ruth since my "explosion," and now some relationship with Ruth became possible for the first time. I was finding pleasure and satisfaction in my work and elsewhere, especially in painting and in my garden, which seemed to be my only positive tie with my mother.

We began to cut down both the length and frequency of the sessions, and to increase the fee at my insistence, and in the summer of 1955 I agreed to finish. Once again I became involved sexually, and unsuccessfully, for again it was an oedipal situation. I went back to D.W. for help and he saw me once a week for about eighteen months, at the end of which he told me plainly that it was time I took over my own responsibilities and got on with my life—"be yourself," but now for *me*, not for him.

CHAPTER 6

Aftermath, 1957–1984

F inishing was not too dif-
ficult: my relationship with D.W. went on as a
friendly and comfortable one though I could never be
part of his closest circle. This was explicit and under-
standable. I could see him or ring him from time to
time if occasion arose, and he invited me to join a
small group meeting to discuss some of his newest
work.

I was no longer a nonperson, my identity being
acknowledged by D.W. and other people; I was established as a training analyst and he referred patients to
me, both adults and adolescents (about whom we did
not always agree) for consultation or analysis, including some about whom he cared specially. My
standing as a painter was also recognized: I was
exhibiting regularly and selling occasionally. I could

be and *do*, asserting myself without undue guilt or anxiety or paranoid reaction. In the words of an old friend from before analysis I was "not recognizable for the same person." ("It seemed that to be known is to have life and continuance in other men's keeping"—Power 1969.)

I have gone on since then in self-analysis (Little 1964b), even recently working over again much of what I have experienced, reconsidering the *value* of the regression, seeing it more clearly, especially the time in hospital as a challenge to determine which would prove the stronger, the sickness or the health, which were both there.

I have had success and failure, pleasure and pain, in both my professional and personal life and have found life worth living as it had scarcely been before. I have been enormously enriched by a relationship, as a woman, with a man of wide interests, brave and loyal and very great fun, whose loss I mourn.

As with any outstanding personality it is only too easy to idealize or to denigrate D.W., to think of him as "charismatic" or a "cult figure," but to do either is to *dehumanize* him, to cling to phantasy and misconception.

For me, ambivalence and anxiety of course remain, for no analysis ever does away with them or is ever complete. In part of myself I still find my unavoidable (and valuable) anger (Winnicott 1963d) in response to the mistakes and things he missed or misunderstood, and in any case they were necessary if I were to grow and to mature (Winnicott 1962b); perfection would have been useless. (He could not give me all that the *infant* me wanted.)

The overriding feeling is one of deep and lasting gratitude, for D.W. enabled me to find and free my "true self" (Winnicott 1960b), my spontaneity, creativeness, and ability to play; he restored my sanity without leaving me "only sane" (Winnicott 1971b). I am in touch with the child in me who wants to play, to use (Winnicott 1968) what she has been given, and resents the demand to "write a nice 'thank you' letter," while my more mature self is endeavoring to express the true thanks I feel by giving this account of his work with me. ("I don't know whether I like it, but it's what I meant," as Vaughan Williams said of his Fourth Symphony.)

CHAPTER 7

Winnicott as a Teacher

This part would be in-
complete without some reference to D.W. as a
teacher. I never experienced him in that "official"
capacity myself, though I learned a great deal from
him in the course of my analysis (I owe him that, too);
and any claim I may have to say that I practiced
anything remotely like it rests there and is not a
matter of imitation or of having been "taught."

I don't think any analyst can always be consciously
aware of what he is doing, and why, *at the time*
("How can I know what I think till I see what I say?"—
Graham Wallas, *The Art of Thought*), and I don't
think D.W. was—he was not afraid to react, or to be
spontaneous, but he often explained what he was
saying or doing, sometimes at the time, and sometimes in a later session. He reviewed his work con-

75

stantly, in self-analysis, and was willing to recognize and to correct a mistake or omission when the patient's material showed the need.

What follows next I have been told. His seminars and supervision sessions were lively and friendly affairs, even when he disagreed with the ideas and methods of others; they were informal, often helped along by mugs of black coffee and ginger biscuits. "He taught you to free-associate *as an analyst* to all your patient's material. When you had told him about it he would lean back, close his eyes, and begin to talk, chuntering away to himself, apparently associating freely, about the patient, about what you had said, anything that had happened. Not criticizing, not asking, 'Why did you say that?' but sharing his associations with you" (Ralph Layland, personal communication). He would illustrate what he said from his own work, discussion was free; he did not "lecture" (it would have been "bad manners"), and he encouraged students or colleagues to find their own individual ways of working, not to follow his, for these belonged essentially and inseparably with his personality.

Though working quite differently, he fully acknowledged his debt to Melanie Klein, and as I said before he used "standard technique" (i.e., Freud's own method, interpreting the transference, especially in terms of repressed oedipal material and the activity of the superego) in cases of psychoneurosis. But there was no class of illness that he considered impossible to analyze, as Freud regarded narcissistic neuroses and psychoses; only some individuals, according to the degree of their illness and their circumstances.

I am sure that his very personal technique could not be taught *by precept.* The direct experiencing of it was all-important for me, and something that was absorbed unconsciously, without words. But apart

from what he has written about his work, something
of the feel and the sense of it can surely be learned by
students in analysis or supervision with analysts who
have themselves an understanding of it on more than
just an intellectual level.

Characteristically, the dedication of one of his
books published shortly before his death, *Playing
and Reality*, reads: "To my patients who have paid to
teach me." The importance of learning from our
patients as a mother learns from her infant was the
cornerstone of his work, for they, not we, are the ones
who know.

II

On the Value of Regression to Dependence

The hunter and the animals he seeks seem to join and become part of one another and of all the life there is.
James Houston, "Spirit Wrestler"

In Part I, I wrote of continued self-analysis after the termination with Winnicott in 1957, and of "reconsidering the *value* of the regression, seeing it . . . especially the time in hospital as a challenge to determine which would prove the stronger, the sickness or the health, which were both there."

This consideration has its validity, but beyond what the experience brought me for myself there is a much wider value: for my own patients, for Winnicott, and for those psychoanalysts who are willing to allow such regression in their treatment of psychotic patients.

CHAPTER 8

The Value of Regression

Except for its concluding section on Winnicott as teacher, Part I was written from the viewpoint of a *patient,* a borderline psychotic. It contains little reference to the theoretical and practical considerations that concern the analyst.

From the analyst's point of view the value of regression to dependence can be stated very simply: *it is a means by which areas where psychotic anxieties predominate can be explored, early experiences uncovered, and underlying delusional ideas recognized and resolved, via the transference/ countertransference partnership of analyst and analysand, in both positive and negative phases.* In practice, of course, it is not so simple.

Winnicott's paper "The Metapsychological and

clinical aspects of regression within the psychoanalytic set-up" (Winnicott 1954b) deals in detail with
the theoretical and practical considerations. He refers
to both transference and countertransference, especially the latter, as being of supreme importance, but
very little in the way of case material is available to us
in any of his writings. My object in writing this
chapter is chiefly to illustrate clinically what he has
written, but also to add something of my own which,
as I will show later, he has acknowledged.

I must make it clear here that I am using the term
countertransference in the strict sense in which I
defined it in my paper "Counter transference and the
patient's response to it" (Little 1950):

> repressed elements, hitherto unanalysed, in the
> analyst himself which attach to the patient in the
> same way as the patient "transfers" to the ana-
> lyst affects etc. belonging to his parents or to the
> objects of his childhood: i.e. the analyst regards
> the patient (temporarily and varyingly) as he
> regarded his own parents. . . .These feelings are
> infantile, subjective, [and] irrational, some plea-
> surable, some painful. [pp. 34–35; see also Win-
> nicott 1960c]

But beyond what is repressed there may be much that
is unanalyzed, that has never been even preconscious,
which belongs to the very earliest levels of the analyst's own experience and so forms part of his countertransference—a part that is intuitive, and of the
greatest importance in the treatment of psychosis.

Regression to the level of the prevailing anxiety
occurs in every patient in analysis as soon as conscious control is relaxed. Apart from analysis it occurs in sleep, in times of leisure, of absence of de-

mand whether from without or from within; and
where anxiety is not intense it can be rewarding as
well as pleasurable, allowing for dreaming, fantasy,
and creativity.

Gavin Maxwell (1968), in his book *Raven Seek Thy
Brother*, describes particularly well what happened
in a regression during convalescence after a serious
accident in which he had sustained multiple injuries:

> There was one curious thing about my convales-
> cence while I was still in the hospital. I was
> working, as soon as I had recovered the energy
> and application necessary to work at all, on the
> autobiography of my childhood, which was pub-
> lished in 1965 under the title of *The House of
> Elrig*. I realized with absolute certainty that my
> helplessness and dependence, my hairless body,
> my reduction in middle age to a childhood sta-
> tus, had performed for me some miracle of time
> transposition, so that I was able to think as a
> child and to recall images and attitudes that
> would otherwise have been lost to me. In some
> sense I did really re-enter childhood, so that to
> write of it was not an effort of memory, but an
> actual reliving of those early years, because I was
> required now to conform to that distant authori-
> tarian pattern. The re-creation was strangely
> complete; I had passed through the stage of acute
> illness, corresponding to the dependent infant
> years, and gone on to impatient and resentful
> convalescence which found its exact parallel in
> the intolerant protest of puberty and adoles-
> cence. In this way and because the sequence of
> the writing followed these stages faithfully but
> unintentionally, long lost scenes and feelings,
> dialogues and mental directions became things

of the present and not of the past. The images, I
suppose, were random, but they were real and
uncontrived. [p. 53]

The care he had received in the "stage of total dependence" had clearly been adequate to his needs then,
and had enabled him to progress to the stage where
he could relive the difficulties of his adolescence and
use the experience creatively. His transference was to
the hospital and to its "authority" and amounted to
no more than what is normally seen in such a situation, relating to conflict and loss; the reliving of
childhood is characteristic of regression.

Disturbances in adolescence are common to most
people, and many are resolved spontaneously. But
where loss, or conflict, either within an individual or
between him and his environment, gives rise to anxiety (psychoneurosis), some psychiatric help may be
needed to make possible a regression such as Gavin
Maxwell describes. "Standard" psychoanalysis, using the technique of verbal interpretation, is appropriate here.

Many people, however, have pockets of what is
called "madness" or "mental illness." These may
extend over large or small areas of someone's personality, causing a greater or lesser degree of disturbance
in his life, his work and leisure, and his relationships.

Such things arise from anxieties earlier than those
of psychoneurosis; they concern survival and identity
(Freud 1917), and for those who suffer from them the
sound of words spoken may be important, but not
their meaning, so that verbal interpretation is of little
use and other means of dealing with the anxiety need
to be found.

For myself, like many others, I was apparently
"normal"; I attended school, college, medical school,

practiced as a GP, and was accepted for training and qualified as a psychoanalyst. I worked throughout my analysis, except for holidays and three short spells of depression. But I suffered enormous anxiety that I had to hide, and was inhibited in many ways, especially in the field of relationships, for I had little self-confidence or sense of my own identity. Ordinary psychoanalysis was unsuccessful and I needed deep regression, to the level of total dependence, from which I have been able to develop, albeit belatedly, to become something of a more real, balanced, and mature person.

In prenatal and early postnatal life an infant is totally dependent, and by the time of birth integration, though begun, is not far advanced; survival cannot be taken for granted. The "unthinkable" or "archaic" anxiety is aroused by traumata "against which an individual has no organized defence, so that a confusional state supervenes." It is experienced as annihilation; being totally destroyed (like a pricked balloon); falling endlessly; having no means of communication and so being totally isolated; being unconnected to one's body; or lost in space (Winnicott 1956b, 1962d).

Later, when identity begins to develop but is not yet established, disturbance can be less painful, the confusion less, and defenses can be rebuilt and strengthened.

Only an environment capable of meeting all needs can ensure survival and promote integration; where this is not provided annihilation anxiety will persist and periods of confusion will follow disturbances and failures.

As a result of his long and intensive study from birth of both healthy and disturbed children and their mothers, and of psychotic patients in regression,

Winnicott came to regard psychosis as an "environmental deficiency disease" (Winnicott 1949a), calling
for a return to the time when the adequacy or deficiency of the environment was all-important. The
analysand relives and reenacts events of that time
and the analyst provides such environment as is
capable of "total active adaptation" for as long as
that is needed, and, later, of gradual de-adaptation.
A "good-enough" environment, "holding" reliably
(Winnicott 1952b; Richard Rowlands [1565–1630?]
"Lullaby"), will support emotional development on
the primitive pattern (Winnicott 1945) of coming
together, becoming a person; finding reality (T. Traherne [1637?–1674] "The salutation") and a capacity
for fantasy (illusion or imagination), creativity, and
forming relationships; and the ability to use symbols
and metaphor (Sechehaye 1951).

Regression to dependence is a "healing process"
(Winnicott 1954b) that originates not in the analyst
but in that part of the analysand, his "true self"
(Winnicott 1949a, 1960b), which can still hope for
reversal of the original failure, through finding in the
analyst enough adaptation to his needs. "Treatment"
is needed, rather than "technique"; and intuitive
behavior and management, not verbal interpretation.
But it is not easy, for it involves the analysand in a
frightening return to the earliest unintegrated state.
There is the risk of repeated annihilation by stimuli to
which he has to react physically (startle reflex), and
with forced integration, against which he has no
defense and which he cannot comprehend; of being
let fall while helpless, there being no boundary or
control.

The analyst has to be able to give up his defenses
against the same anxiety, the dread of annihilation, of
loss of identity, both for himself and for his patient. At

the same time his own identity must remain distinct and his reality sense unimpaired, keeping awareness on two extreme levels, reality and delusion. He is in the position of a mother *vis-à-vis* her infant, but where neither he nor his patient is in fact in that situation. This calls for the same qualities as those of a "good-enough mother" (Winnicott 1952b), empathy with the infant on his level (Winnicott 1960a), and ability to see him as a separate person. Not relying on his "professional attitude," to accept a "direct relationship" (Winnicott 1954b) with him as distinct from the mirror image, and remembering that sexuality has no meaning here; psychically to merge with him, accepting the delusion of oneness with him; to tolerate his hate without retaliating when the original traumata are relived (Winnicott 1947, 1960c) and to stand his own feelings when they are aroused.

The analyst's "evenly suspended attention" (Freud 1913) seems here, to me, to be close to the "primary maternal preoccupation" described by Winnicott (1956a): perhaps it is basically the same thing, though less in degree, for the primary maternal preoccupation apparently means an element of temporary regressive, even schizoid, illness in the mother.

There are many difficulties in the way for both partners. Time is essential; and absence of disturbance by physical illness, demands of the outside world, work, etc.; but above all there is in each the internal resistance due to the anxiety itself. Management is necessary. The analytic setting provides physical comfort, warmth, quiet, and absence of interruption in general. Emotional comfort too is found in the analyst's attitude of acceptance, encouragement, and response, which may be active at times, or more often neutral. In a severely disturbed patient

these are absolute *needs* (Winnicott 1949a,b,
1954a,b), not wants; and when they are met they
have interpretative effect, like the "cues" that a
mother gives to her infant.

As he is not an infant he reacts to failures in an
adult way, with an adult body, so there is danger. For
the analysand there is a risk of failure if his needs are
not met, of rebuilding defenses, flight into illness or
sanity; or suicide, which he must be free to choose if
he wishes, so destroying the analysis. For the analyst
there is serious danger of being attacked either when
the anger aroused by the original trauma is released,
or when tension lessens and he makes a mistake that
cannot be used. It is a matter of life and death,
somatic or psychic, and if the analyst did not survive
through illness, accident, or attack (or developed a
countertransference psychosis), there could be no
recovery for the analysand, only at best a return to
the *status quo ante.*

Where both survive the danger points, and defenses are not rebuilt, the analyst can gradually
withdraw his adaptation; the analysand can come
together and become a person, a self that is different
from the "self" that was there before (though related
to it). The experience of being "mothered" is truly
mutative in that it resolves the anxiety concerning
survival and identity by providing reassurance and
continuity of being. Awareness of being real, recognition of what is inner or outer, ability to fantasize and
to distinguish fantasy from reality, to symbolize, to
relate to others in a way that was previously impossible, and to mature, first to the "depressive position"
(Klein 1935) or "stage of concern" (Winnicott, 1950,
1963a), and later to the oedipal level, follow as in
normal development, helped on by whatever maturity had been achieved before.

It is not always recognized that the dependence is

mutual. The analyst depends on his patient to attend his sessions, to pay, to cooperate as and how he can; to allow himself to regress and become helpless; and to grow. The analyst cannot do these things for him, or make him do them; he can only facilitate them by his reliability and by his understanding and ability to communicate on the patient's level.

Every successful analysis of a psychotic or border-line patient is so much clear gain for him. But for the analyst, over and above the satisfaction of having done a useful piece of work and satisfied a shared desire, there is gain in greater understanding of psychosis and greater knowledge of himself. Beyond this again is the wider value to psychoanalysis as it is developing, and to the outside world.

CHAPTER 9

Exploring Psychotic Anxieties

I was lucky, in 1949, to find or be found by (which on the delusional level is the same thing [Little 1957b, 1960b]) a psychoanalyst who for the previous twenty years had been treating psychotic patients.

I could gradually relinquish my omnipotence and false, "caretaker" self and, relying on his "holding," relive my traumatic infancy and childhood. Eventually I could imaginatively destroy and be destroyed by him (again the same thing) and later, finding we both survived, could use him and be of use to him (Winnicott 1968, 1970b).

D.W. was aware from the beginning that my prevailing anxiety concerned survival and identity, and at the same time that in other areas I had achieved a fair degree of maturity. It was on this understanding

that he based his diagnosis and his decision to undertake my analysis.

In the first hour I shut him out, by hiding under the
blanket and saying nothing, and a few days later I ran
away from the analysis into a sexual relationship for
which I was not really ready. I think this was an
unconscious attempt to avoid the despair I tried to
make him recognize by smashing a vase in his room.
D.W. was not yet ready to meet this destructive
acting-out and left me alone with the chaos I had
created, so the sense of futility and hopelessness
remained.

Not long after this came a session in which I
presented an apparent reliving of a traumatic birth
experience, confirming his recognition that I was "in
an extremely infantile state" (Winnicott 1949a,b) and
that if normal emotional development were to be
made possible deep regression would be needed,
possibly even to prenatal life.

I have come to regard this session, with its recur-
rent spasms of bodily tension rising to a climax and
followed by relief, as a reliving of prenatal experience
rather than of a traumatic birth. (Much recent work
has confirmed that the sensory apparatus is fully
developed at birth. Repeated disturbances in prenatal
life through somatic manifestations of the mother's
anxiety—rapid heartbeat or respiration, increased in-
testinal movements, etc.—transmitted through the
amniotic fluid, stimulate reactions in the fetus—
sudden waking from sleep, movement, etc., and are
apparently experienced as what could be called "annihilation." The birth process will then represent a
repetition in exaggerated degree of the annihilation
and discontinuity that had already been experienced
[Winnicott 1949b].)

My actual birth was easy; my mother delivered

herself before the arrival of doctor or midwife. I
suspect that she delayed sending for them partly
because of her belief that "if you don't think about it
the pain will go away" and partly because of fear lest
the midwife should hold back the head. (She had
experienced this as an act of "cruelty" in her previous delivery and never understood the need for it.)

During her third pregnancy, she told me, she was
"almost suicidal" with anxiety.

It is not possible to think of my mother as being
capable of any degree of "primary maternal preoccupation." This is not at all to say that the coming child
was not important to her—only that she could never
think of it except as part of herself and that the very
idea of separateness aroused anxiety, as to her it
meant annihilation.

The lifelong anxiety that made my mother "chaotic" and "unpredictable" (Winnicott 1961) persisted,
of course, after delivery. It took the form during my
infancy of continual disturbances of my still largely
unintegrated state. She told me that whenever she
found an infant's mouth open she would close it, and
she would remove a sucked thumb from the mouth; if
the infant lay on its back or left side she would turn it
to lie on the right "so as to prevent pressure on the
heart" (the ribcage meant nothing to her). Body
orifices were constantly investigated; later, nightly
enemas were given (and in adolescence there would
be long sessions of squeezing "blackheads" and acne
pimples). Like a small child, she could leave nothing
alone.

Misunderstandings such as her fear of the midwife
led to disasters, whether for herself or for her family,
so chaos always threatened. I was scolded for being
"a baby" or "thin-skinned" if I made any "fuss"
when startled, and I could defend against it only by

withdrawing, holding myself (Winnicott 1954a) (as in
my first session with D.W.), or by identifying with her
and sharing the primary delusion of oneness with
her: the delusion that became apparent in my transference to D.W.

To me D.W. did not *represent* my mother. In my
transference delusion he actually *was* my mother
(Winnicott 1954b), and as there is in reality continuity between mother and fetus, genetic and bodily
(via the membranes and placenta), so to me his hands
were the umbilical cord, his couch the placenta, and
blanket the membranes, all far below any *conscious*
level until a very late stage. Delusion was never
mentioned—I recognized it much later myself—but
by his behavior he tacitly accepted it, meeting me on
that level but at the same time maintaining his own
maturity and reality.

Through his reliable "holding" (Winnicott 1952b)
and acceptance of a direct relationship, I began to
trust D.W. and to find continuity and something of a
"mutual feeding situation" (Winnicott 1970b). Such
a situation had been actively prevented in my infancy, for I was bottle-fed, rolled tightly in a shawl so
that no limb movement was possible. The hole in the
teat was so small that milk could be got only by dint
of real hard work, a new teat being fitted as soon as
the hole was enlarged. (I saw this same thing ten
years later, when my brothers were infants, and later
still I was astonished to hear a pediatrician at Great
Ormond Street Hospital advise a free flow of milk
through a teat with a large hole, and to see him
demonstrate it.)

Such interferences with feeding led to failure of
communication between my mother and me; rocking
and rhythmic movement (Winnicott 1956a) were pre-

vented early, but encouraged in the toddler stage.
There *was* important communication through her
singing to me, especially in my bath; she had a
beautiful soprano voice and enjoyed singing nursery
rhymes, nonsense, opera, etc. This, with her sense of
humor and love of gardening, are lasting positive ties
with her, and together with my father's stability they
probably prevented my becoming totally insane. But
other developments of our relationship failed.

Her interferences alternated with disregard, and
excessive attention with "dropping," for she was
continually being distracted. What mattered one
minute was totally unimportant the next, and what
was important to me had to be set aside. This remains
as a negative tie; for I still experience any disturbance
when I am preoccupied as if my mother were once
more taking possession of me. I recover, but it takes
time!

Communication with D.W. became possible
through the long silences, and this unconscious two-
way stream later led both to the writing of my papers
and to some development in his work. But even in the
analytic hours there were disturbances. In those
times of silence D.W. would become drowsy, fall
asleep, and "twitch," and I would react openly with
rage as I had so often raged inside myself at my
mother. More seriously, chaos threatened with his
two coronaries, his depression, divorce, remarriage,
and move of house.

Already, throughout the succession of therapies,
chaos was always round the corner. My first therapist
(Dr. X) repeatedly answered telephone calls in my
sessions; Miss Sharpe's heart condition posed a constant threat, and chaos did supervene when she died.
Marion Milner, to whom I went then, helped to restore

some stability and I rebuilt defenses, but the change again from her to D.W. was yet another threat. My defense was to run away, but it soon broke down.

Chaos came again when after my "explosion" at my mother in 1952, over something entirely trivial, she came back with a demand on me that made it clear once more that I and all I had—my body, my clothes, money, etc.—were hers to dispose of as she wished, not for support, which I would willingly have given.

My reaction was rage, which I then discharged against my own body, as if it were hers. I suffered an accident resulting in a long period of immobility, followed by a lasting confusional state—virtually a regressive illness—culminating in hospitalization during D.W.'s summer holiday in 1953. My only alternative to accepting this would have been to break off the analysis, but I was by then far too aware of my need for help to be able to do so, and after a violent protest I agreed to it.

Again, my attempt to be unintegrated for a time was defeated in the hospital; a series of interruptions (all kindly intended) repeated for me the original prenatal and postnatal traumata. I was overwhelmed by chaotic feelings, which I discharged in an orgy of smashing. But it was a place where I could react violently without actually destroying or being destroyed by it. In the locked ward to which I was taken I *could* be unintegrated, and then find continuity both in myself and in the outside world. I decided finally to live. I was no longer delusionally dependent on bodily continuity or identity with D.W.; I could be separate at last from my mother and find my health stronger than the sickness that originally was hers, and with which I had been identified (Little 1957b).

I have often wondered (and I am not alone in this)

whether putting me in hospital could have been
avoided in any way, and I know now that it could not.
But this can be understood only when all the circumstances and the kind of care I received there and from
D.W. himself are considered.

I was already 52, and my life as a psychoanalyst
was not yet well established. My mental state was
such that I was deeply regressed in every session and
only coming together slowly afterward. Notes that I
have of that time show the intensity of my anxiety
and my extreme reaction to any disturbance. I
needed to be unintegrated throughout my holiday,
and in particular to be protected from any possible
interruption by my mother, who was still a real
source of potential danger to her own life and mine.
(Sadly, she died six months later; she made a sudden
rush to go downstairs, my sister could not catch her,
and she fell, fracturing her femur. It was pinned, but
kidney failure followed.)

D.W. was nearly 60; he had suffered two coronary
thromboses and was always at risk of further illness.
His holiday was due. The analysis in which he was
deeply "engaged" (Fordham 1960) was a great strain
on him in every way—time, energy, anxiety, emotion;
it had already lasted four years and could apparently
go on indefinitely.

It was a crisis point, literally a matter of life and
death, both mine and D.W.'s. If he did not survive
then neither could I, psychically at least. To that
extent we were as nonseparable as a baby and mother
(Winnicott 1952b).

He chose the hospital carefully; he consulted be-
forehand with the Medical Superintendent, whom he
knew, and was disappointed to find him away on
holiday when the time came. D.W. took me there
himself and left full notes for the Deputy Superinten-

dent. Throughout the five weeks of my stay he telephoned the hospital and wrote to me every few days.
Care was taken that letters from my mother did not
reach me. Finally, he fetched me home.

I have written at length about the hospital in Part I.
It was a place where internal pressures could safely
be released more freely than in the consulting room
in the space of analytic hours. The different sur-
roundings and different personnel gave me an opportunity to form "transitional" (Winnicott 1951) relationships, while D.W.'s constant contact provided the
necessary continuity in the transference relationship
with him.

I was enabled to live an infancy and childhood of
my own, as distinct from living or reliving my mother's for her. Through reaching the earliest levels of
what is sometimes called "the paranoid-schizoid position" in a controlled, safe, nonretaliatory and rea-
sonably consistent setting, I arrived at a new starting
point from which I could develop to the "stage of
concern" and later to the oedipal situation—eventually to my chronological maturity. My psychotic and
nonpsychotic areas were firmly joined together.

The later stages of the analysis, which still lasted
another four years, were certainly considerably
shorter than they would otherwise have been. Anxieties concerning survival and identity were no longer
important; the character of the sessions was different;
they now dealt verbally with depressive, and later
oedipal anxiety.

Having had this experience I could now know
something of mental illness from inside, and the
strengthening effect of it was immeasurable. I could
find my own personal way of meeting some of the
needs of my patients. I could face failures without
being destroyed by them, and successes without

becoming omnipotent. This was the further value for me.

For Winnicott, the value was that his own self-knowledge was increased through his continual self-analysis; his already developed understanding of psychosis was widened and supported. He found material on which to test out existing ideas and to base new ones (learning from me [Winnicott 1971b, Dedication]), and later he used it extensively in writing and speaking, both in England and elsewhere, to many different audiences to whom also it was worth a very great deal.

CHAPTER 10

Stolen from Mother's Handbag

To sum up: I started from the statement that regression to dependence is "a means by which areas where psychotic anxieties predominate can be explored, early experiences uncovered, and underlying delusional ideas recognized and resolved, via the transference/countertransference partnership . . . in both positive and negative phases."

To demonstrate this, I have given an account of my own analysis with Winnicott. I have shown the origins of my psychosis in experiences of my mother's "state of organized chaos" (Winnicott 1961) before and after my birth. My delusion was of total oneness, identity, and continuity with my mother, which I then transferred to Winnicott, with all the ambivalence belonging to it; for me he *was*, absolutely, my

107

mother's womb. I had at some time to discover that in
reality he was not; that he and I were not identical, or
continuous; nor was he a part of myself that I projected. I could not make him be any of this except in
fantasy; he came to be outside the "area of my
omnipotence," and objectively perceived (Winnicott
1968).

And yet, I could find the grain of truth that is
behind every delusion. With my mother there was
real continuity, genetically and (in prenatal life) physically, via the placenta and membranes, and there
was actual two-way interchange through the amniotic fluid and umbilical cord. After birth there was
perceivable body contact and some relationship,
though limited.

So with Winnicott, psychically, there was genetic
continuity—we had in Freud a common psychoanalytic progenitor; he and I had absorbed the same
ideas, and there could be true two-way interchange
on that level.

He was very well aware of his countertransference
and could use it positively, in reliable-enough "holding" and care of me and in direct relationship with
me. His objective hate (Winnicott 1947) could be
discharged in calling for payment, taking holidays,
etc., but above all in putting me into hospital. He met
me psychically on my every level, including that of
the delusion itself. This was represented in bodily
form in the actual holding of my hands "like an
umbilical cord," as I have described it (in fact, my
paper " 'R'—the analyst's total response to his patient's needs" is based on what I learned in this way
[Little 1957a]).

But finally, much later, I found something of his
intuitive countertransference that may still perhaps
not have been fully conscious.

In 1969 he read a self-revealing paper (since pub-

lished) entitled "D.W.W. on D.W.W.," at a meeting
that I attended (Winnicott 1970a). In it he discussed
the various influences on his work from his school-
days up to that time: he referred to his father, to
Darwin, Freud, Klein, and many others. He ended
with a reference to "Margaret Little's use of the
delusional transference concept," saying that this
was something that he had needed and had "got from
somebody else, *almost as if I stole it out of my
mother's handbag.*"

Here, surely, he showed himself communicating
with me, learning from me, and acknowledging our
affinity. He gave me full and generous recognition of
a contribution to his work that I am proud to have
been able to make in my papers, especially "On
delusional transference" (Little 1957b), and "On
basic unity" (Little 1959). This apart from my analysis, though they derived from it, as he well knew.

But what is "mother's handbag" but a familiar
symbol or metaphor of her womb (Oscar Wilde, *The
Importance of Being Earnest*)? And could there be a
more beautiful illustration of my statement at the
beginning about the importance of transference and
countertransference in the psychoanalytic treatment
of a psychotic or borderline patient through regression to dependence? I am indeed grateful for it!

A Note on Donald Winnicott

In September 1971, I was asked: "A summary of the place of Dr. Winnicott's work and its relation to the total field is much needed. Can you be persuaded to write it?"

I said that I would try, but that it could not be done quickly. By the time I had written what I could, it was already too late and could not then be published, but surely it is still relevant.

These terms of reference, of course, would set any writer an impossible task, and I do not take them too seriously, but I have considered what is called for—not an obituary, eulogy, or memoir, but some kind of assessment—an objective recognition and statement.

It is simply not possible for *anyone* to make something that takes D.W.W. only as an "objective object." Some element of perceiving him as a "subjec-

113

tive object" (his own expressions) inevitably comes in, in anyone who was in any way associated with him, especially for those who (like myself) were his analysands, and our assessment must depend on the degree to which we have become able to perceive both him and ourselves objectively.

Regarding him, then, as an objective object does not rule out a personal element. If it did, we would end up with something fossilized or mummified, nonbeing, to which *no* feeling could attach, and this would automatically destroy the very assessment that we are trying to make.

Winnicott once referred to himself as "an isolated phenomenon" (an historical reference in his paper on his relation to Melanie Klein and her work). He developed the concept of an individual that is implicit in this, speaking (in his paper "On Communicating," etc.) of "the individual's use and enjoyment of modes of communication, and the individual's non-communicating self, or the personal core of the self that is a true isolate."

We have, then, to consider him both as communicating and noncommunicating, and the interplay between these two aspects of him, of his readers, fellow-workers, analysands, etc., and to recognize that anyone as much an individual as he could not but strike sparks of one kind or another.

It follows that he is easily both idealized and seen as bedeviling whatever he touched—psychiatry, psychoanalysis, pediatrics, and so forth.

Either attitude does him a gross injustice; in fact, those of us who mainly approve or agree also have serious points of difference with him, while those who mainly disagree or disapprove often find themselves, however reluctantly, accepting what has hitherto seemed to them outrageous. Perhaps the chief outcome of this is the very width of his impact on the "total field," where ideas that he first put forward have been quietly appropriated and accepted without being attributed to him, and often attributed elsewhere. Things that he reached without tub thumping or ostentation often fall into place, suddenly "clicking" somewhere, and references to his sayings turn up in all kinds of unexpected places (like a reference in an article on school architecture in one of our national Sunday newspapers). He had quite a special ability to make himself understood by all kinds of people, to say things that could not be put into words, and to get in touch with the creative elements in people, i.e., with the really well part of a personality below the surface.

But where what he has been saying has not "clicked" (often because it has not yet been fully developed,often because it is really obscure, or because he assumed that people understood when they didn't), it is, of course, experienced as puzzling and frustrating.

I am indebted to a colleague for a report of a particular example of this which occurred in 1968, in New York, when Winnicott read his paper "On the use of an object and relating through identification." In it he speaks of "destruction of the object," meaning this to be understood as *imaginative*, not actual.

Failure to grasp this led to an outbreak of violent hostility among his audience, and rejection of his ideas and his work in general. It was particularly unfortunate that he was seriously ill at the time, and quite unable to reply then, but the paper was later included in *Playing and Reality* (1971b).

The effect was extremely damaging, and has persisted in certain areas to the present time. The hostility will continue for a long time yet, until more people understand his meaning, and realize that he did not claim to have said the last word on this, or any other matter!

Attempting to test his work, his discoveries, or his idiosyncrasies, or to make comparisons with other workers—Freud, Klein, Sechehaye, Hartmann, etc.— would be fruitless at this point, but I want to consider some particular topics that seem to me outstanding, apart from some of the more obvious ones such as "primary maternal preoccupation," "transitional objects," "squiggle technique," etc.

First of all is his capacity to stand paradox and ambivalence, knowing them to be inherent in life itself, without seeking ways around, defenses against, or avoidance of them. This capacity grew and developed in him, an ongoing process throughout his professional and personal life, not steadily continuous, but varying in scope and speed ("Human beings are jerky"), and people have speculated how one could *live* with so few defenses.

Out of this came such things as his recognition of the importance of being able to refuse; the need (whether for child or adult) for "no" as well as "yes" and for frustration at the right time as growth promoting, where at the wrong time it is growth inhibiting; the importance of "confrontation" on occasion; the value of destructiveness and of the parent's or therapist's ability to survive it; and many other truths about men, women, children, and adolescents *as real people*.

Not long before his death he began to develop completely new ideas on the origin of creative activity in the earliest, two-sided, undifferentiated, preambivalent, pre–object-related stage of development in which, paradoxically, destruction is creative of both self and object. This is the stage of "being," and of nothing-else-at-all, which depends upon survival being guaranteed by the environment, so that annihilation anxiety can safely be ignored and the self *come into being* as a "true isolate."

There have been many former postulates, e.g., Aquinas's "I am psyche-soma," Descartes' "cogito ergo sum." But these are surpassed by the importance of "I am" (long known as the forbidden holy name of the Omnipotent Creator) and finally of the still simpler statement "I," which postulates and includes, but does not state, "not I."

Even this is not new; it is the "Ancient of Days," the "Spirit brooding over the face of the waters"— "One is one and all alone, and ever more shall be so." What *is* new is Winnicott's recognition and use of it, and it is not only new but individual and personal to him, as expressed in his understanding of Hamlet's"To be, . . . or . . ." (pause) "not to be? *That* is the question."

Somewhere about here he died, in a way, although he was still exploring, writing, lecturing, seeing patients, etc. But for him dying was an essential part of his life, which would have been meaningless and incomplete without it, something he had to reach at the right time.

He failed us, of course, by not knowing everything, or not communicating all he knew; but how awful if he had!

Many different people have described Winnicott as "a genius," and I think their meanings are as varied as the people themselves. Ralph Vaughan Williams defined a genius as "the right person in the right place at the right time," and I think this fits Winnicott. But here it is left to others, especially the many who will come later, to discover him and his work *for themselves* (see his statement to the effect that others before him had found the same things, including Freud, but that what mattered was that *he* had found them for himself).

I am indebted to Dr. Virginia Suttenfield, whose only direct contact with Winnicott had been at a colloquium in Paris. She told of his informal conduct of it—in shirt-sleeves, talking a little, sitting back tilting his chair, everyone else talking, and he finally gathering together, summing up all the contributions, commenting, and expressing personal thanks. Later, in a teaching session, one of her own students stumblingly told her how much she had helped him. To her this was the direct outcome of her sensation of Winnicott's living, ongoing quality. "He was a *yeasty* person," she said.

POSTSCRIPT

Yes—he *was* a genius—not of the same order of magnitude as Newton, Einstein, Shakespeare, Beethoven, etc., but he did the same thing that each of them did—he *shed light,* on the importance of the early environment in particular, treatment of psychosis, origins of creativity, value of destructiveness, etc., and opened the way for others to develop these themes further.

Nature and Nature's laws lay hid in night.
God said "Let Newton be"! and all was light.
                                    Alexander Pope,
               Epitaph intended for Sir Issac Newton

But light is meaningless without darkness, as creativity is meaningless without destruction. And we cannot ignore the dark things in D.W.W.'s life and work—in his sadness at being unable to father (or mother) children. His mistakes, failures, tragedies even. Errors of judgment; omnipotence perhaps; and at the end of his life letting down patients about whom he cared deeply, simply by dying. (For one he was his third analyst to die.) D.W.W. had written (1954) of the *need* for the analyst to survive for psychotic or borderline patients to recover. We tend to overlook both the nature of the patients with whom he was working, and that we know nothing of the content of their analyses.

In 1950 I wrote, "Each of us has his private grave-yard, and not every grave has its headstone." This is still true. D.W.W's record cannot be fully revealed as yet. We have only our memories, and further assessment can only come later. Even Newton, Einstein, etc., are still being re-assessed in the light of later knowledge. D.W.W. will stand his ground in the long run, and his *yeast* will live and grow for a long, long time.

Like him, others will succeed, and fail, and psychoanalysis, which he valued above all, will change and grow in ways we cannot foresee.

This book is concerned with Winnicott's "true self in action" in many aspects, and it is appropriate here to refer to *The Spontaneous Gesture—Selected Letters of D. W. Winnicott. The Spontaneous Gesture,* edited by F. Robert Rodman (Rodman 1987), reflects Winnicott's spontaneity, generosity, and openness, his "true self in action." The content is mainly a selection of letters written by D. W. Winnicott to a wide variety of people. One important letter (No. 43, pp. 71–74) shows Winnicott's endeavor to persuade both Melanie Klein and Anna Freud to lessen their bitter rivalry and to work instead for the progress of psychoanalysis and for the welfare of the Society to which both belonged. The repercussions of this struggle became well known in the outside world and have persisted to some extent to this day.

Winnicott's own disagreement with Melanie Klein concerned at first the *manner* of her presentation rather than its *matter*; specifically, he drew attention to a certain rigidity and stylization of the language ("Kleinspeak"—my words, not his) used by her and her associates (No. 25, pp. 33–37), which led to discomfort in meetings, increasing the separation between the various elements in the Society.

Later, more theoretical differences arose. In particular, there was the question of the importance of the environment in early infancy (but also in the life of an analysand) and her emphasis on "inborn" hereditary factors, determining the presence at birth of "envy," which to him was something too sophisticated to be present in a neonate (No. 73, p. 120; No. 102, pp. 157–161).

Very few of the letters are part of an ongoing correspondence; in this sense, the greater number are clearly spontaneously motivated. To many colleagues Winnicott wrote about papers presented by them or others—agreeing, disagreeing, commenting, raising other points. To Melanie Klein and Joan Riviere he wrote protesting at their attitude of disparaging his contributions and implying that mental illness in him prevented him from acknowledging Klein's superiority in every respect. He asked for a "response" to "gestures" he had made (No. 25, pp. 33–37; No. 59, pp. 94–97).

He wrote understandingly to mothers asking for advice concerning their children. He would suggest that they might find solutions to the difficulties within themselves and their families, and that no absolute "right" or "wrong" could be known. Others asked about the therapeutic value of psychoanalysis and were told that it varies with the individual—

many it helps, others cannot use it; it is not a cure-all.

Spontaneity also relates importantly to courage, self-confidence, and truth to self, to independence of thought and action, and to originality. And it was this very independence and originality, shown particularly in his paper "Metapsychological and clinical aspects of regression within the psycho-analytical set-up," read in 1954, which brought him into his sharpest conflict with Klein and members of her group. Disregarding Winnicott's observations of infants, Klein held that a much greater degree of ego development is present at birth—and a degree of instinct development—than he could agree to. In accordance with this view, she insisted that only verbal interpretation of transference is of any therapeutic significance. Later, from there, she developed her theory of "inborn envy" and its essential link with a death instinct and with heredity, which again Winnicott could not accept. (Rodman does not mention that in 1962 Winnicott gave a talk entitled "A personal view of the Kleinian contribution" to Candidates of the Los Angeles Psycho-Analytical Society, in which he made clear that he regarded it as being of very great importance.)

In a talk entitled "Sum, I Am" given to the Association of Teachers of Mathematics, Winnicott claimed:

> In my own job *I do know something*, and I have expertise and I have accumulated experience. In the areas of mathematics and of teaching I am a *greenhorn.* . . . My job is definitely to be myself. What bit of myself can I give you, and how can I give you a bit without seeming to lack wholeness? [Winnicott 1968a]

Unfortunately Rodman has misunderstood Winnicott's paper on regression to dependence and the treatment of psychosis (1954), where Winnicott stresses the importance of "management as the method" and "the transference/countertransference alliance as the essential instrument of change," but this does not destroy Rodman's contribution. He has shown us a different aspect of Winnicott's true self in action and succeeds, in fact, in giving "a bit" without losing sight of Winnicott's essential "wholeness."

To finish, I would like to share with my readers two poems that for me show almost literally Winnicott's own pictures of an "ordinary devoted mother," and of a child's early emotional development: his progressive discovery of his own body, himself, and his world, as Winnicott described them, and as he gave to me, and enabled me to discover for myself.

I do not know whether Winnicott himself knew them in any literal sense of the word, but they could never have been far from his unconscious knowledge.

Lullaby[1]

Upon my lap my sovereign sits
And sucks upon my breast;
Meantime his love maintains my life
And gives my sense her rest.
  Sing lullaby, my little boy,
  Sing lullaby, mine only joy!

When thou has taken thy repast,
Repose, my babe, on me;
So may thy mother and thy nurse
Thy cradle also be.

---

[1]"Lullaby," by Richard Rowlands (1565–1630?). From *The Oxford Book of English Verse.*

Sing lullaby, my little boy,
Sing lullaby, mine only joy!

I grieve that duty doth not work
All that my wishing would;
Because I would not be to thee
But in the best I should.
  Sing lullaby, my little boy,
  Sing lullaby, mine only joy!

Yet as I am, and as I may,
I must and will be thine,
Though all too little for thyself
Vouchsafing to be mine.
  Sing lullaby, my little boy,
  Sing lullaby, mine only joy!

The Salutation[2]

These little Limbs,
  These Eyes and Hands which here I find,
This panting Heart wherewith my Life begins;
  Where have ye been? Behind
What Curtain were ye from me hid so long?
Where was, in what Abyss, my new-made Tongue?

When silent I
  So many thousand thousand Years
Beneath the Dust did in a Chaos lie,
  How could I Smiles, or Tears
Or Lips, or Hands, or Eyes, or Ears perceive?
Welcome ye Treasures which I now receive.

---

[2]"The Salutation," by Thomas Traherne (1637?–1674). From *The Penguin Book of English Verse*. In music, "Dies Natalis," by Gerald Finzi (1901–1956).

I that so long
Was Nothing from Eternity,
Did little think such Joys as Ear and Tongue
To celebrate or see:
Such sounds to hear, such Hands to feel, such Feet,
Such Eyes and Objects, on the Ground to meet.

From Dust I rise
And out of Nothing now awake;
These brighter Regions which salute mine Eyes
A Gift from God I take:
The Earth, the Seas, the Light, the lofty Skies,
The Sun and Stars are mine; if these I prize.

A Stranger here
Strange things doth meet, strange Glory see,
Strange Treasures lodg'd in this fair World appear,
Strange all and New to me:
But that they mine should be who Nothing was,
That Strangest is of all; yet brought to pass.

References

Fordham, M. (1960). Countertransference symposium. *British Journal of Medical Psychology* 33:1–8.

Freud, S. (1913). On beginning treatment (further recommendations on the technique of psycho-analysis). *Standard Edition* 12:121–145.

——— (1917). *Introductory Lectures on Psycho-Analysis. Standard Edition* 16.

Klein, M. (1935). A contribution to the psychogenesis of manic-depressive states. In *Love, Guilt and Reparation and Other Works 1921–45*, pp. 262–289. London: Hogarth/Institute of Psycho-Analysis, 1975.

Little, M. (1945). The wanderer: notes on a paranoid patient. In *Transference Neurosis and Transference Psychosis: Toward Basic Unity*, pp. 3–31. New York: Jason Aronson, 1981.

——— (1950). Countertransference and the patient's response to it. In *Transference Neurosis and Transference Psychosis: Toward Basic Unity*, pp. 33–50. New York: Jason Aronson, 1981.

——— (1957a). "R" —the analyst's total response to his patient's needs. In *Transference Neurosis and Transference Psychosis: Toward Basic Unity*, pp. 51–80. New York, Jason Aronson, 1981.

———— (1957b). On delusional transference (transference psychosis). In *Transference Neurosis and Transference Psychosis: Toward a Basic Unity*, pp. 81–91. New York: Jason Aronson, 1981.

———— (1959). On basic unity. In *Transference Neurosis and Transference Psychosis: Toward a Basic Unity*, pp. 109–125. New York: Jason Aronson, 1981.

———— (1964a). Transference in borderline states. In *Transference Neurosis and Transference Psychosis: Toward a Basic Unity*, pp. 136–153. New York: Jason Aronson, 1981.

———— (1964b). Transference/countertransference in post-therapeutic self-analysis. In *Transference Neurosis and Transference Pyschosis: Toward a Basic Unity*, pp. 247–263. New York: Jason Aronson, 1981.

Little, M., and Flarsheim, A. (1964). Toward mental health: early mothering care. In *Transference Neurosis and Transference Psychosis: Toward a Basic Unity*, pp. 167–181. New York: Jason Aronson, 1981.

Maxwell, G. (1968). *Raven Seek Thy Brother*. Longmans Green/ Harmondsworth: Penguin, 1974.

Power, R. (1969). *The Hungry Grass*. Bodley Head, quoting an unknown source.

Rodman, F. R. (1987), ed. *The Spontaneous Gesture—Selected Letters of D. W. Winnicott*. Cambridge, MA: Harvard University Press.

Sacks, O. (1985). *A Leg to Stand On*. Duckworth.

Searles, H. F. (1959). The effort to drive the other person crazy— an element in the aetiology and psychotherapy of schizophrenia. In *Collected Papers on Schizophrenia and Related Subjects*, pp. 254–283. London: Hogarth, 1965.

Sechehaye, M. (1951). *Symbolic Realization*. New York: International Universities Press.

Sharpe, E. F. (1930). The technique of psychoanalysis. In *Collected Papers*, pp. 9–106. London: Hogarth, 1950.

———— (1943). Cautionary tales. In *Collected Papers*, pp. 170–180. London: Hogarth, 1950.

Thompson, F. (1924). "Ode to the Setting Sun." In *Collected Poetry*. Burns, Oates and Washbourne.

van der Post, L. (1982). *Yet Being Someone Other*. London: Hogarth.

Winnicott, D. W. (1945). Primitive emotional development. In *Through Paediatrics to Psycho-Analysis*, pp. 145–156. London: Hogarth/Institute of Psycho-Analysis, 1975.

_____ (1947). Hate in the countertransference. In *Through Paediatrics to Psycho-Analysis*, pp. 194–203. London: Hogarth/Institute of Psycho-Analysis, 1975.

_____ (1948a). Paediatrics and psychiatry. In *Through Paediatrics to Psycho-Analysis*, pp. 157–173. London: Hogarth/Institute of Psycho-Analysis, 1975.

_____ (1948b). Reparation in respect of mother's organized defence against depression. In *Through Paediatrics to Psycho-Analysis*, pp. 91–96. London: Hogarth/Institute of Psycho-Analysis, 1975.

_____ (1949a). Mind and its relation to the psyche-soma. In *Through Paediatrics to Psycho-Analysis*, pp. 243–254. London: Hogarth/Institute of Psycho-Analysis, 1975.

_____ (1949b). Birth memories, birth trauma, and anxiety. In *Through Paediatrics to Psycho-Analysis*, pp. 174–193. London: Hogarth/Institute of Psycho-Analysis, 1975.

_____ (1950). Aggression in relation to emotional development. In *Through Paediatrics to Psycho-Analysis*, pp. 204–218. London: Hogarth/Institute of Psycho-Analysis, 1975.

_____ (1951). Transitional objects and transitional phenomena. In *Through Paediatrics to Psycho-Analysis*, pp. 229–242. London: Hogarth/Institute of Psycho-Analysis, 1975.

_____ (1952a). Psychosis and child care. In *Through Paediatrics to Psycho-Analysis*, pp. 219–228. London: Hogarth/Institute of Psycho-Analysis, 1975.

_____ (1952b). Anxiety associated with insecurity. In *Through Paediatrics to Psycho-Analysis*, pp. 97–100. London: Hogarth/Institute of Psycho-Analysis, 1975.

_____ (1954a). Withdrawal and regression. In *Through Paediatrics to Psycho-Analysis*, pp. 255–261. London: Hogarth/Institute of Psycho-Analysis, 1975.

_____ (1954b). Metapsychological and clincial aspects of regression within the psycho-analytic set-up. In *Through Paediatrics to Psycho-Analysis*, pp. 278–294. London: Hogarth/Institute of Psycho-Analysis, 1975.

_____ (1956a). Primary maternal preoccupation. In *Through Paediatrics to Psycho-Analysis*, pp. 300–305. London: Hogarth/Institute of Psycho-Analysis, 1975.

_____ (1956b). Clinical varieties of transference. In *Through Paediatrics to Psycho-Analysis*, pp. 295–299. London:

Hogarth/Institute of Psycho-Analysis, 1975.

_____ (1960a). The theory of the parent-child relationship. In *The Maturational Processes and the Facilitating Environment*, pp. 37–55. London: Hogarth, 1965.

_____ (1960b). Ego distortion in terms of true and false self. In *The Maturational Processes and the Facilitating Environment*, pp. 140–152. London: Hogarth, 1965.

_____ (1960c). Counter-transference. In *Maturational Processes and the Facilitating Environment*, pp. 158–165. London: Hogarth, 1965.

_____ (1961). The effects of psychotic parents on the emotional development of the child. *British Journal of Psychiatric Social Work* 6:12–20.

_____ (1962a). Ego integration in child development. In *Maturational Processes and the Facilitating Environment*, pp. 56–63. London: Hogarth, 1965.

_____ (1962b). Dependence in infant-care, in child-care, and in the psycho-analytic setting. In *Maturational Processes and the Facilitating Environment*, pp. 249–259. London: Hogarth, 1965.

_____ (1962c). Communicating and not communicating leading to a study of certain opposites. In *Maturational Processes and the Facilitating Environment*, pp. 179–192. London: Hogarth, 1965.

_____ (1962d). The aims of psycho-analytical treatment. In *The Maturational Processes and the Facilitating Environment*, pp. 166–170. London: Hogarth, 1965.

_____ (1962e). A personal view of the Kleinian contribution to the theory of emotional development early stages. In *Maturational Processes and the Facilitating Environment*, pp. 171–178. London: Hogarth, 1965.

_____ (1963a). The development of the capacity for concern. In *The Maturational Processes and the Facilitating Environment*, pp. 73–82. London: Hogarth, 1965.

_____ (1963b). Morals and education. In *The Maturational Processes and the Facilitating Environment*, pp. 93–105. London: Hogarth, 1965.

_____ (1963c). From dependence towards independence in the development of the individual. In *Maturational Processes and the Facilitating Environment*, pp. 83–92. London: Hogarth, 1965.

_____ (1963d). Psychotherapy of character disorders. In *The*

Maturational Processes and the Facilitating Environment, pp. 203–216. London: Hogarth, 1965.

———— (1963e). The mentally ill in your case load. In *Maturational Processes and the Facilitating Environment,* pp. 217–229. London: Hogarth, 1965.

———— (1963f). Psychiatric disorder in terms of infantile maturational processes. In *The Maturational Processes and the Facilitating Environment,* pp. 230–241. London: Hogarth, 1965.

———— (1965). *The Maturational Processes and the Facilitating Environment: Studies in the Theory of Emotional Development.* London: Hogarth/Institute of Psycho-Analysis.

———— (1968). The use of an object and relating through identifications. In *Playing and Reality,* pp. 101–111. London: Tavistock, 1971.

———— (1968a). Sum, I am. In *Home is Where We Start From.* New York: Norton.

———— (1970a). D.W.W. on D.W.W. Unpublished.

———— (1970b). The mother-infant experience of mutuality. In *Parenthood,* ed. J. Anthony and T. Benedek, pp. 245–256. New York: Little, Brown and Company.

———— (1971a). Creativity and its origins. In *Playing and Reality,* pp. 76–100. London: Tavistock.

———— (1971b). *Playing and Reality.* London: Tavistock.

———— (1972). Fragment of an analysis. In *Tactics and Techniques in Psychoanalytic Therapy,* ed. P. Giovacchini. New York: Science House.

———— (1975). *Through Paediatrics to Psycho-Analysis.* London: Hogarth/Institute of Psycho-Analysis.